# Runes For Beginners

*Your Complete Beginner's Guide to Reading Runes in Magic and Divination*

**Vivienne Grant**

# © Copyright 2019

# All rights reserved.

The content contained within this book may not be reproduced, duplicated or transmitted without direct written permission from the author or the publisher.

Under no circumstances will any blame or legal responsibility be held against the publisher, or author, for any damages, reparation, or monetary loss due to the information contained within this book. Either directly or indirectly.

Legal Notice:

This book is copyright protected. This book is only for personal use. You cannot amend, distribute, sell, use, quote or paraphrase any part, or the content within this book, without the consent of the author or publisher.

Disclaimer Notice:

Please note the information contained within this document is for educational and entertainment purposes only. All effort has been executed to present accurate, up to date, and reliable, complete information. No warranties of any kind are declared or implied. Readers acknowledge that the author is not engaging in the rendering of legal, financial, medical or professional advice. The content within this book has been derived from various sources. Please consult a licensed professional before attempting any techniques outlined in this book.

By reading this document, the reader agrees that under no circumstances is the author responsible for any losses, direct or indirect, which are incurred as a result of the use of information contained within this document, including, but not limited to, — errors, omissions, or inaccuracies.

# Table of Contents

Introduction .................................................. 6
Chapter 1: History of Runes ............................. 12
   Elder Futhark ........................................... 13
   Odin, son of Borr and Bestla ........................ 16
Chapter 2: Runes and Power ........................... 20
   Sayings of the High One ............................. 20
   Becoming a runemaster .............................. 23
   Understanding the Runes ........................... 24
Chapter 3: Runes of the Elder Futhark ............. 26
   The First ætt, or Freyr's Aett ....................... 27
   The Second ætt, or Heimdall's Aett .............. 49
   The Third ætt, or Tyr's Aett ......................... 66
Chapter 4: The Art of the Runestave ................ 83
   Creating a Runestave ................................. 84
   The Hammer Rite ...................................... 88
   Ritual of Formation ................................... 91
   The use of cards ........................................ 93
   Paper runes .............................................. 94
   Casting the runes ...................................... 99
   Containing the runes ................................. 99
   Theal's Stool ............................................. 100
   Understanding your Runes ........................ 100
   Meditate on the runes ............................... 104
Chapter 5: Runecasting for Beginners ............. 106
   One-Rune Layout ..................................... 107
   Two-Rune Layout ..................................... 110
   Three-Rune Layout .................................. 111

Four Directions Layout ...................114
　　Five-Rune Layout ..........................117
　　The Persona ................................120
　　Runic Cross .................................123
　　The Mirror....................................126
　　The Seven Rune Layout................131
　　Mimir's Head...............................135
　　Beginner's Tips ............................141
Chapter 6: Advanced Runecasting
Techniques..........................................145
　　The Four Quarters.......................146
　　The Tree of Life ...........................149
　　The Cosmos .................................154
　　Celtic Knight Cross ......................160
　　The Futhark.................................166
　　The Airts Method .........................173
　　Worldstead Layout ......................181
Chapter 7: Discovering more about the
runes ...................................................192
　　Meditating With the Runes..........192
　　Norse Mythology and Symbolism.................194
　　Elemental Links ...........................195
　　The Nine World for Beginners.....198
　　Tips to be successful with Divination ..........202
　　Final thoughts..............................207
Bibliography.......................................209

# *Introduction*

All living things communicate.

The rich, marine life forms inhabiting the water that covers roughly 71% of the Earth's surface communicate with each other. Avian creatures also have their own ways of communication. Even plants have a unique way of communication as they disperse chemical signals to other plants closeby.

However, the human communication system is the most complex among all living creatures on Earth. For one, it involves language, which is a system of sounds, written symbols, and gestures.

In fact, it is safe to say that humans are the only species currently capable of using this complex system unless you have spotted an animal in the wild secretly honing its penmanship. If you have, you've made quite the discovery.

Since no such animals have been discovered, we can safely assume humans have solely evolved with the ability to transform their thoughts, ideas, and messages into written words.

But is that the only thing that makes human language unique?

Not quite. The following are some distinct characteristics that you should know about the human language.

## *Displacement*

The language that we use every day can talk about or describe things that are not present, visible or in close vicinity. As a human, it is simple to ask questions like – "Where is the location of the restaurant?" or, "Where do I put this incredible book when I am done reading it?"

We humans also have the capacity to communicate about objects, entities, or people that we are not sure exist in the real world. For example, we can express our opinions on ghosts, The Avengers, parallel dimensions, Sauron and his dark army, or the fate of any of the characters on Game of Thrones.

Animals do not have this ability. However, scientists know that bees have some form of displacement. When they discover a source of food, they head back to their colony and perform a wiggle-dance to communicate with the other bees and tell them the location of the food source. A minor form of displacement can also be found among ants and ravens. However, this is nothing compared to the ability that we humans possess.

### *Creative*

The human language gives us the power to create. It is possible because we can use a different combination of words to express unique meanings or ideas. Today, it is still debated how many words are in the English language, with some sources such as the Oxford English Dictionary assuming that the official number is close to 750,000.

Any other creature on Earth does not have the capability to communicate like this. Yes, dogs bark, bears roar, and dolphins click. But they have a limited – or closed – systems to communicate, where they can only communicate a single idea. They cannot combine their vocalizations to express themselves or give meaning to things.

### *Recursive*

This characteristic of human language means that we can add new words, phrases, or even entire sentences to other existing words, phrases, and sentences.

For example: "John was playing."

We can extend this further by saying: "Alex saw that John was playing."

It does not have to stop there. We can take it one

step further and say: "Alex saw that John was playing with his bicycle."

If you think about it, you could extend that sentence even more. Of course, this depends on your grasp of the language. But no matter your language strength, with practice, it is possible. Animals, on the other hand, do not have the advantage of recursiveness in their communication.

These set of distinct traits have helped humans develop language in unique ways. This uniqueness has helped humans spread languages into different forms, resulting in dialects, scripts, symbols, and in some cases, even signs.

Evolution and society have made our communication skills superior to any other creature on this planet. While this may seem like a boast, it really isn't, as this is a fact established by scientists and linguists.

According to Ethnologue, a catalog of languages published by SIL International, headquartered in Texas, United States, as of today, there are more than 6,500 languages spoken in the world. That is an astounding number as it would be challenging to name even 100 of them!

Imagine trying to find these languages on our

planet. How many languages are there in one country? After all, there are just about 195 countries in the world today. This expansion of languages shows a spectacular level of diversity.

But this diverse collection of languages developed over time, across millenniums. As various cultures and societies began to develop, they began to form their own languages. Thousands of years ago, as humans drifted to different parts of the world, languages developed their unique forms.

If we look through the history of languages, we will realize that the origin of languages might forever remain concealed. This is due to the disparities between various views from anthropological, biological, genetic, and archeological standpoints. Additionally, we do not have all the proof yet. So, the best we can do is make an estimate.

However, what is certain is the fact that these languages not only spawned other languages, but also the idea of recording them in one form or another.

This is where the uniqueness of human language plays a vital role. You see, the variety of languages led to the evolution of scripts and alphabets. These scripts and alphabets presented their own forms of communication by blending history, culture, and beliefs.

Scripts involved writing and that led to various writing systems. There is the cuneiform, a system of writing developed by the Sumerians. Also, you have the Egyptian hieroglyphs, dominating Egypt's writing and made famous by Hollywood and pop culture.

And then, you have runes, which are also made famous by pop culture.

Human communication created languages, which in turn molded into various forms based on geographical locations. As humans were already proficient in cave paintings since prehistoric times, they could easily develop writing systems to accommodate alphabets and scripts.

Runes are the product of the ingenuity of human communication.

But what makes them extraordinary? How are they linked to magic and the prediction of the future? Before we delve into that, let's look at their illustrious history.

## *Chapter 1: History of Runes*

Runes are a set of alphabets, just like the alphabets that exist in the languages practiced today. They prominently feature vertical and often slanted lines. This arrangement of lines serve a purpose, and they are:

1. Parchments were an expensive commodity back then, so writing on them was not a viable option. Ink wasn't cheap, and for that reason, using it was uncommon. Therefore, runes were carved into objects and surfaces instead.

2. Since carving was used, using straight lines was much easier than curves.

3. While using straight lines, runes avoided the inclusion of horizontal strokes, as those lines could look like the natural lines of surfaces like wood, thereby removing any trace of the line itself.

No one can establish with absolute certainty when the runes originated. One of the most popular theories is that it was developed by the Goths, a race of East-Germanic people.

Historians also believe that runes have taken inspiration from the Latin alphabet. While this does not narrow down its time of origin, it gives a rough estimate, placing it in the 1st century BC.

## **Elder Futhark**

The following are the three main divisions of runes:
1. Early Germanic, also known as Common Germanic
2. Anglo-Saxon
3. Nordic

Out of these three, we will be looking at the Early Germanic script, as that will be the focus of our runic interpretations and much of the work that we will be doing with runes.

This script had 24 letters divided into three groups. Each group, called ættir, consisted of the simple application of math – eight alphabets.

The first six alphabets sounded like f, u, th, a, r, and k, giving the alphabet its distinct name: futhark.

Then came the Roman Empire.

Yes, the very same empire that – at the peak of its power in 117 AD – controlled an area of more than 4 million square kilometers. But before they reached this level of control, they first had to conquer.

As the Roman Empire was in its conquest stage, it spread Christianity to different parts of the world. During the time, the religion used the Latin scripture Volgate, whose letters gained dominion over many languages and scripts as the Romans gained more land.

This eventually led to the diminished use of other alphabets, including Elder Futhark.

However, runes did not die out completely. Their use continued through the dark ages, most commonly used by the Pagans.

As with any language that gets adopted by another culture - or group of people in this case - Elder Futhark went through a slight reformation. It is still unclear why it happened, or even exactly when, but the runic alphabet lost 8 of its letters, eventually becoming the Younger Futhark.

At this point, one might assume that in its new form, the language began to spread to countries far and wide, expanding its use and knowledge. Sadly, that is not what happened to Younger Futhark.

The newer version of the runic alphabet could not

outrun Christianity, as the religion spread fast and far into Scandinavia and Germania. When the religion began to replace paganism in various parts of the world, it did not adopt the Younger Futhark alphabet, eventually leading to the alphabet's demise.

However, back when the runes existed and Christianity hadn't placed its influence on them, they were carved on to many surfaces.

Throughout history, you will discover runes inscribed on a number of objects, from swords and war tools to jewelry and gemstones, and even on common materials like stone.

This begs the question: do we know what object had the earliest runic inscription?

As a matter of fact, we do. However, if you were expecting the inscription to be present on swords, gemstones, or any such exotic items, you might be a little disappointed.

The truth is, the earliest runes were found on a comb.

That's right. The Vimose Comb, discovered in Vimose, Denmark, bears runic alphabets that read "harja". Though the meaning of the word is still debated, many scholars believe that the word could mean either "comb", which would be the obvious meaning, or "warrior", which would be an odd word to appear on a comb, unless this particular comb belonged to one.

The comb is part of a collection of objects from Vimose that date back to circa 200 to 300 BCE. These objects are collectively known as "Vimose inscriptions".

But if runes can be rooted in history, what about their mystical properties? Well, you should know there are no confirmed reports on when or where runes originated.

And this brings us to Norse mythology.

## Odin, son of Borr and Bestla

While historians today still debate the origins of runes, the Norse people had no doubt where it came from.
It all began with the Alfadir, or Allfather, Odin.

You see, Odin had a strong thirst for knowledge and wisdom, and would go to any lengths to gain them. If you've watched the Thor movies or read mythology, you will have realized that Odin is often depicted with one eye. Although the movies show him wearing an eyepatch, we can safely assume that it has probably just been added for the sake of entertainment.

The missing eye of Odin is a testament to the Norse god's sacrifice to know more, as he gave up the eye to sip from Mimir's well, imbuing him with the knowledge from the cosmos.

And that's just one example of his extreme acts.

According to Norse mythology, the great tree of Yggdrasil occupies the center of the cosmos. The rest of the universe surrounds the tree and its branches reach into the Nine Worlds.

At the base of the tree is the Well of Urd, whose limitless depths hold some of the most powerful forces and beings in the universe. Among these beings lie the Norns, three maidens who possess the ability to control the fates of all creatures in the world.

This ability essentially makes them quite powerful, even more so than the gods themselves, as all beings, including the gods, are tied to the fates.

One of the ways that the Norns decide the fates of all entities is by carving runes into Yggdrasil. Once the runes are carved, the tree sends the inscribed fates across the cosmos and into the Nine Worlds.

Of course, this came to the attention of Odin, who envied the Norns and craved the knowledge of the runes. As you might have guessed, at this point, he once again went to excessive measures to get what he wanted.

It is important to note that the runes do not reveal themselves to anyone. They pick those who are worthy to receive their knowledge. Odin was aware of this, and in order to prove his strength and sacrifice, he hung himself from the Yggdrasil tree, pierced himself using a spear, and gazed into the Well of Urd.

For nine days and nine nights, he hung from the tree, balancing between life and death. During those nine days, he commanded the other gods and entities not to come to his aid.

It was then, after the final night, that he began to notice symbols in the well.

At last, the runes had revealed themselves to him!

With this newfound wisdom and power, Odin was able to perform incredible feats; he could heal any physical and emotional injury, render his enemies helpless, banish malevolent magic, raise the dead, cast protective spells on his friends and allies, bind people to him, and more.

And this is how the runes came into existence in

our world.

After they came into existence, people and cultures began to use them in divination, to perform magic, foresee the future, or cast blessings and curses. As time went on, more and more people became aware of their forms and began to utilize them in their rituals and practices.

Today, this power is available to you. And you won't have to hang from a tree and pierce yourself with a spear to get it.

## *Chapter 2: Runes and Power*

### Sayings of the High One

The Hávamál, or the "Sayings of the High One" - a single poem that is part of an entire collection of Norse poems – speaks of trying to seek and interpret the signs of the runes which were hidden to the world back then.

In the poem, the seeker of runes is asked a series of questions:

Do you know how to write?

Do you know how to read?

Do you know how to paint?

Do you know how to prove?

Do you know how to ask?

Do you know how to offer?

Do you know how to send?

Do you know how to spend?

There are many ways to interpret the above questions. However, most believe that the questions are meant for those seeking to understand the runes. It is a way to gauge the wisdom of the runemasters, or runecarvers - people who are specialists at using runes.

Instead of trying to understand each question's meaning, it is better to group the questions together and gain deep knowledge of their intent.

In the first group, we will include the first three questions.

Do you know how to write?

Do you know how to read?

Do you know how to paint?

This practically exposes the basic understanding of runes; the ability to read, write, or paint them. The idea behind these questions is to encourage the runemasters to ask themselves whether they truly know the runes, their meaning, and how to turn them into a written script or carve them if necessary. The word 'paint' does not literally indicate the act of painting, but rather the act of inscribing or embedding runes into surfaces.

Let's move on to the next group of questions.

Do you know how to prove?

Do you know how to ask?

These two questions are hard to understand because each one on its own might be confusing to interpret. However, put together, you might notice the warnings presented in them. The questions simply ask runemasters to pay attention to what they ask of the runes. The word "prove" questions the runecasters' skills. In other words, are they confident of their abilities? The word "ask" is the act of using the runes and focusing on the practical abilities of the runecaster, where they ask the runes to reveal their knowledge.

Think of the words "prove" and "ask" as the science and art of working with runes.

The science represents the knowledge of the runes and the art emphasizes the experience of the runecaster.

Finally, let's move on to the last set of questions.

Do you know how to offer?

Do you know how to send?

Do you know how to spend?

It is widely believed that these questions are a form of reminder. They indicate the act of giving, represented by the word "send", and the act of making a payment, highlighted by the word "spend".

Runecasters commit to the act of giving. If someone approaches runecasters to seek knowledge, they should be aware of the act of giving. This is because giving someone knowledge is a powerful act, so runecasters must decide just how much knowledge to provide.

The act of spending is understanding the value of the knowledge. It decides just how much runecasters must receive in return for the knowledge they provide.

You might be aware of the old adage: power corrupts.

You might also be aware of another one: knowledge is power.

Runecasters must understand that with their abilities and the knowledge they can provide, they could ask for a high payment. However, one must absolutely not resort to greed or swindle.

## Becoming a runemaster

History places many runemasters in the 11th century. Runemasters were wise men or women who belonged to a tribe or priests and priestesses with the ability to read and create runes. While not much is known about their practices, it has been discovered that they usually resorted to materials such as wood, which was widely available, to carve runic symbols.

Today, you can find runes inscribed on materials of different sizes and shapes, from plastic to gemstones. Once you understand runes, you might be able to create your own carvings using your skills and own set of materials.

## Understanding the Runes

As there were no specific written accounts of their details until Christianity began to spread, we have to rely on manuscripts that date back all the way to the 9th century, during the advent of the Christian era. These manuscripts feature poems, where each rune has a separate verse. The verses begin with the runic alphabet, followed by their name.

The unique arrangement of alphabets of the Elder Futhark into three ætts (a word which roughly translates to either "families" or "groups") might help scholars understand the relationship between the runes. However, the meaning behind the entire pattern remains a mystery. Researchers use a combination of history and Norse mythology as a guide to understanding them. They hope to gain more insight into how the Norse might have used runes to form a deep connection between the spiritual and real world.

So, with much investigation and research, we have quite a bit of knowledge about them. This is the knowledge that will be made available to you.

# *Chapter 3: Runes of the Elder Futhark*

Finally, fellow runemasters, we are going to start to gain an understanding of the runes themselves. Each rune has its own meaning, and you can use them in the upright or reverse positions, similar to how you would use a Tarot card. However, with runes, you are connecting your physical presence to the spiritual world.

When interpreting runes, you will be faced with two positions. The first is the original position, which reveals its own set of meanings. The second is the reversed position, showing negative implications. When reversed, some runes will look the same. In such cases, there are no reverse meanings attached to the rune.

With that in mind, let's begin.

# The First ætt, or Freyr's Aett

In this section, we will look at the aett of Freyr, or Freyja, or Freya. It includes the runes Fehu, Uyuz, Thurisaz, Ansuz, Raido, Kenaz, Gebo, and Wunjo.

In Norse mythology, Freya is one of the most prominent goddesses. She was originally a Vanir, one of the two primary forms of deities featured in mythology, with the other being the Aesir. Eventually, after a war between the two forms of deities, she became a member of the Aesir.

Freya is commonly known as the Goddess of Love. However, she is also associated with beauty, sex, fertility, gold, war, death, and lust.

## *Fehu*

ᚠ

Literal Meaning: Cattle

Divination Meanings: Wealth, prosperity, money, promotion, and goals.

Phonetic Equivalence: f

Pronunciation: fay-who

Magic Usage: Finding money, achieving goals, finding a job, and gaining promotion.

The Vikings used to believe that owning cattle signified success, wealth, and money. It was a status symbol, as the more cattle you owned, the more power you had in society. While this tradition might have died down over the ages, the idea behind Fehu remains the same; that of possessions, power and wealth. As such, it indicates either the abundance of financial strength in the present or the presence of financial wealth in the near future. The power aspect comes from owning more wealth, leading to the growth of said power.

However, the rune also calls for us to be secure in our physical situation. We can apply this sense of security to what we have right now. After all, while we can gain possessions over time, we should also ensure to protect the ones we own.

Fehu reminds us that, just like cattle, we must not aim to spend our day-to-day lives in the same routine. We should seek out more than what is currently available and possible in our lives. We should strive to aim for better. In this sense, Fehu is a sign of hope.

Fehu speaks about the responsibility of having wealth and possessions, referring especially to the act of sharing it with others. In many ways, it highlights the importance of giving to our fellow man and the social success that follows such acts.

As the rune also links to fertility, it could indicate pregnancy now or in the near future.

### *Reverse Fehu*
This position typically indicates the loss of possessions or of something precious. It could be a physical object, your status in society, or anything that you have struggled to keep. It could also be the loss of strong relationships with family, friends, or loved ones.
As Fehu links to fertility, it could indicate a failed pregnancy. Alternatively, this failure can refer to a lack of creative process.

## *Uruz*

ᚢ

Literal Meaning: Auroch, a form of wild Ox

Divination Meanings: Vitality, passion, sexuality, instinct, and wildness

Phonetic Equivalence: u

Pronunciation: oo-rooze

Magic Usage: Strengthens will, boosts sexual stamina and energy, and assists in hunting

Uruz lies in stark contrast to the representations of Fehu. This is because Uruz is associated with the auroch, a type of wild Ox that was once found all across Europe but is said to have been extinct since the 17th century. The aurochs displayed wild and untamed power, which is in opposition to the tame and calm behavior of cattle. In essence, the rune represents the wildness of man. A sense of physical strength. An indication of untamed power. You can also see this in its idea of the masculine power of Oxen.

Through these symbolic references, runecasters can interpret this as opportunities for great power and health.

Additionally, as opposed to your ordinary cattle, aurochs were animals capable of carrying large loads. As such, the rune represents the idea that you might be carrying a great load in the present, or will encounter a burden in the future, but you are able or will be able to shoulder it, despite what anyone thinks.

You might encounter unexpected changes, and while changes are usually disconcerting, in this case, you might not have any cause for concern, as you will experience a welcoming shift. However, an auroch is a strong animal and one cannot push it against its will. Therefore, be careful how much force you use when a favorable situation presents itself.

When it comes to matters of sexuality, the rune could represent the awakening of sexual desires.

### *Reverse Uruz*
This reveals a sense of weakness or, alternatively, the domination of your life by others. It could express sickness, but it does not have to be constrained to physical maladies. When you see this rune, it is a good idea to take note of one's diet, mental health, stress levels, and other emotional and physical parameters of health.
The rune speaks of brutality or violence that may

occur to the individual, or it may be the individual who inflicts it upon others.

Remember that when the Uruz speaks of opportunities, one should not miss them as they are typically life-changing. If lost, they might never present themselves again. That's why the reverse Uruz indicates that something valuable that could have been yours is now probably lost forever.

## *Thurisaz*

þ

Literal Meaning: Giant, or thorn

Divination Meanings: Focus, knowledge, discipline, and hardships

Phonetic Equivalence: th (as pronounced in the word "thesis")

Pronunciation: thoor-ee-saws

Magic Usage: Assisting in meditation and learning, clearing bad situations, and attaining self-discipline.

Thurisaz is part of a set of 'obstacle' runes. Now, when we see the word obstacle, we immediately keep our guard up. We expect trouble, danger, and probably even a degree of tragedy. But the obstacles indicated by this rune refers to challenges that are placed in our lives to improve us, add strength to our character, and give us perspective.

It is akin to a complex math problem with many parts, with each part a representation of Thurisaz. To get the result, you have to tackle each section individually.

This rune is a way to predict that such obstacles will appear in our near future and allows you to prepare for them.

Thurisaz is commonly associated with the Norse god Thor who is believed to have an aggressive personality. With this aggressiveness, however, comes a strong sense of defensiveness. This means that while Thor would attack with vehement force, he was also known for his strong defensive tactics.

Hence, when combining the rune's penchant for predicting obstacles and Thor's personality, we can ascertain that we may encounter problems in the future and should be ready to defend against them.

Furthermore, the rune recommends that you do not take any drastic or hasty action in the present. This is because the structure of your life, relationships, and other factors are likely to change without warning, rendering your actions useless. You must rather focus on letting go of the things from the past if they still hold sway over you.

This rune also presents itself as a reactive force. Your life may involve navigating a maze of relationships, both business and personal. Thurisaz warns you about these relationships.

Perhaps you need to keep an eye on your business partners, your co-workers, or employees. Perhaps you will need to handle rivalries, dissatisfaction, or jealousy within your family, your circle of friends, or your loved ones. Whatever the scenario, you must react to these situations, but ensure that you protect yourself as well.

## *Reverse Thurisaz*

It is no surprise that when positioned right side up, the Thurisaz encourages you to defend yourself against an oncoming problem because the reverse reveals a sense of defencelessness due to a situation you could not prepare for.

It also reveals a harmful, and perhaps evil intent from someone you know. This person might be spreading disinformation about you. If you are aware of anyone who could be capable of such an act, it is best to either defend yourself or deal with the situation as diplomatically as possible.

## *Ansuz*

ᚨ

Literal Meaning: Odin

Divination Meanings: Leader, balance, and shaman

Phonetic Equivalence: a (as pronounced in the word "ball")

Pronunciation: awn-sooze

Magic Usage: Ability to lead, make wise decisions, and assist with divination and magic

This rune, sometimes referred to as the "God rune", has strong connections to Odin. Norse mythology represents Odin as a god of war and wisdom. This duality is what highlights the balanced nature of the rune.

Similar to Odin gaining the wisdom of the runes from the Well of Urd, Ansuz represents the idea of gaining wisdom from languages. This wisdom allows us to be more effective in communication.

The presence of this rune shows the immediate need for communication to take place, whether that happens with our family, friends, business associates, or loved ones. It may allow us to simmer down any conflict, disagreement or misunderstanding. However, the need for communication is not merely to oversee a troubling affair. It is a sign that you might need to build something with an individual or a group of people. It is a chance for you to enhance your relationship, your standing, or even your status through productive communication.

The rune gives you the power to understand signals, even those that appear in the form of revelatory messages. If it wasn't for the rune informing you to be aware of them, these signals might have passed you by without your knowledge. It is similar to a road sign, showing you how much distance remains until your destination so you know when you are reaching.

Ansuz also predicts the presence of a guide. It is unclear how this guide might assist you. The person could provide assistance, directly influencing your task. Alternatively, the individual could be there for moral support, giving you much-needed motivation when you require it.

### *Reverse Ansuz*
This position could signify a problem with

communication. It could be due to a physical problem where you might have trouble communicating effectively because of illnesses. It could also be due to a failure to get the messages across, leading to misunderstandings.

You could also experience ignorance from other parties. People might not return your calls or messages. They might not answer your requests. Sometimes, your attempts at communication might not be successful.

Example: You could be attempting to call someone during a sudden crisis, and because of technical reasons, you might not be able to reach them.

## *Raido*

ᚱ

Literal Meaning: Wheel

Divination Meanings: Journey, destiny, pilgrimage, progress

Phonetic Equivalence: r

Pronunciation: rye-though

Magic Usage: Guarding travelers, and bringing new changes

Raido is symbolic for travelers, both for their physical journey and for the journey they take to improve their lives. The presentation of this rune indicates a new experience. Such an experience could be a trip to a different country or discovering novelty in an existing location.

When it comes to the journey of life, this rune links itself to the complex tapestry of relationships that we form. Think of these relationships as a web. As we encounter new people, we add new strands to this web.

When this rune shows itself, it could reveal a new addition to this web of relationships that you maintain.

Alternatively, it explores the idea of a journey you may be taking in your life that could change you. For example, you could have decided to start meditating to bring more peace to yourself. That is a journey, but that journey is riddled with challenges. However, the rune shows that just like the wheel, you need to keep pressing forward. This is because while the journey might be challenging, it may eventually prove to be rewarding.

You might undertake lifestyle changes, spiritual journeys, and new habits. These endeavors may test your mettle, but know that the results are worth the efforts.

### *Reverse Raido*
Alas, things might not be the way you want them to. Your journey might end abruptly. There are greater chances for you to take an unwise decision. You might also have plans interrupted by sudden changes or occurrences.

From your relationship standpoint, you might have unexpected additions to your web, some of whom you might not welcome.

## *Kenaz*

〈

Literal Meaning: Torch or flame

Divination Meanings: Enlightenment, wisdom, creativity, and inspiration

Phonetic Equivalence: c (as pronounced in the word "car")

Pronunciation: kane-awze

Magic Usage: Creating inspiration, aiding in studies, and removing fear and anxiety

The Kenaz is a feminine rune, supporting the facets of hope, mystery, and influence. If a woman draws the rune, she can expect love from a man to enter her life soon. If a man draws the rune, then this is the best time for him to send his love to the women in his life.

The flame is a symbol that has a two-pronged meaning.

The first is the availability of knowledge. Whatever knowledge you have acquired in your life, now is the best time to use it. For example, if you are looking for a new job, you can use the experiences you have gained so far to attempt to try and apply for a better position or role. Another example would be school exams. If you are going to take your exams soon, then the presence of this rune indicates that you might do well.

This rune is also a reminder that if knowledge is not used, it merely remains passive. If you have been hesitant in the application of knowledge, the appearance of Kenaz should prompt you to rethink your apprehensions.

The second meaning refers to flames of passion. The rune speaks of a chance to rekindle the flame with your loved one or discover passion with someone whose compatibility matches yours.

Fires were a way for the ancient man to keep predators away. In life, these predators take the form of fear and anxiety. The rune suggests that now would be a good time to overcome your fears as the opportunities beyond them are plentiful.

### *Reverse Kenaz*
This could reveal the loss of a relationship with someone, whether that person is a friend, family, loved one or acquaintance.

The rune could also indicate the feeling of being exposed or naked. This vulnerability might keep you in your current position and prevent you from moving forward.

There could also be possibilities of minor illnesses or physical and mental problems.

## *Gebo*

X

Literal Meaning: Gift

Divination Meanings: Offering, present, relationship, love, partnership, marriage

Phonetic Equivalence: g (as pronounced in the word "gift")

Pronunciation: gay-boe/yee-boe

Magic Usage: Making or offering a gift, improving or strengthening a relationship, bringing fertility

Until now, the runes we encountered spoke of the connections we have with ourselves. Even when talking about relationships or people, the previous runes spoke about them from the perspective of how they will benefit us. They had an outsider's point of view.

Gebo is the first rune that directly focuses on the connection between people.

That's why when this rune appears, we can deduce that someone might require our help in the near future. When the request arrives, we should not refuse it, even if it means that we may have to make sacrifices on our part. This selfless act might add to our karma, eventually helping us in the future when we might require it.

This is the right rune to draw if you are participating in charitable causes, aid enterprises, or social work. This way, all the selfless help - or contribution in other words - that you perform might be successful. Moreover, these contributions will multiply the number of favors, help, and assistance that you may receive in the future.

Here, an important point to keep in mind is that your help, contributions, and generosity must be true and selfless, and you must not have ulterior motives.

### *Reverse Gebo*
This rune does not have a reversed position.

## *Wunjo*

ᚹ

Literal Meaning: Glory or Joy

Divination Meanings: Rewards, success, bliss, and recognition

Phonetic Equivalence: w

Pronunciation: woon-yo

Magic Usage: Attracting motivation, bringing success to projects, and completing a task

As Wunjo is the last rune of the first aett, it indicates the end of a cycle but the beginning of another one. This end and rebirth cycle makes Wunjo a positive rune to draw.

Its positivity attracts happiness to your life. Also, it suggests marital bliss and domestic contentment, brings harmony in a relationship, and fosters a strong fellowship.

This rune also suggests the appearance of good news and positive well-being.

If you have been seeking success in your endeavors, Wunjo is an appropriate rune to draw. It could highlight the recognition of your worth or the influx of money from success in your work.

The rune recommends projects to have realistic goals to bring more satisfaction to your life.

### *Reverse Wunjo*

A reverse position could indicate alienation, which is brought about by the lack of trust that could arise in relationships or with business partners. Alternatively, you could feel alienated because of conflicts that you have no control over. It suggests that you should probably rethink major decisions that you might be about to make as sudden changes are likely to occur.

There could be a tendency for you to be over-emotional about something, leading to depression or a lack of appetite. Approach any situation with a clear head to avoid a negative impact.

## The Second ætt, or Heimdall's Aett

This section will focus on the aett of Heimdallr, or Heimdall. It includes the runes Hagalaz, Nauthiz, Isa, Jera, Eihwaz, Pertho, Algiz, and Sowulo.
Thanks to Marvel, we might associate Heimdall with the ever-charming Idris Elba. While the movies have embellished certain facts, they did get a few details right.

Among them, the most important idea that was rightly represented in the movies is the fact that Heimdall sat atop the Bifrost, a rainbow bridge that led to Asgard.

Heimdall requires minimal sleep. He can see hundreds of miles away in the day or at night. His hearing is so developed that he can hear the grass growing in fields and hair growing on sheep. So, apart from having some cool superpowers, Heimdall's Aett includes some interesting runes.

## *Hagalaz*

ᚺ

Literal Meaning: Hail

Divination Meanings: Misfortune, disaster, devastation, and hardship

Phonetic Equivalence: h

Pronunciation: haw-gaw-laws

Magic Usage: Disrupting damaging habits or patterns and expelling unwelcomed influences.

This rune focuses on the idea of regeneration.

It predicts that there could be changes in your life that you have no control over. You might experience damages that are physical, emotional, or psychological from forces that are beyond your control. While there is nothing you can do to avoid it, the rune predicts that you might "regenerate" from these experiences. In other words, you will encounter short-term distress to reap long-term rewards.

You might also feel a sense of completion, either from a project that you have been working on or from a personal endeavor.

Hagalaz could also indicate the need for spiritual guidance in your life. Therefore, it is a vital tool used in meditation and relaxation techniques.

### *Reverse Hagalaz*

This rune does not have a reversed position.

## *Nauthiz*

ᚾ

Literal Meaning: Need or Necessity

Divination Meanings: Personal needs, poverty, hardship, irritation, and self-protection

Phonetic Equivalence: n

Pronunciation: now-these

Magic Usage: Attracting destiny and accomplishing a difficult task

The main purpose of this rune is to indicate that you may need to practice patience. If an opportunity that might seem too good to be true presents itself, then it most likely is. Think before you act, however tempting the offer or potential rewards may be.

Take this time to understand your capabilities and limitations as these might help you keep your dreams realistic.

Most of all, be aware of your immediate needs and requirements as they are linked to your physical and mental well-being.

The pursuit of grand trophies is seductive, but it

might distract you from the important things in life. Your family is an example of what is important to you.

Nauthiz also exercises the significance of being reliant on yourself. Seeking help sounds like a sound option, but it might complicate things rather than make things easier for you.

### *Reverse Nauthiz*
When you see the rune in reverse, it indicates the presence of stress and frustration. Here, the idea is for you to deal with these hindrances before venturing further on your journey.

The rune warns you of any "get-rich-quick" schemes or other shortcuts to success as they might land you in deep financial troubles.

## *Isa*

|

Literal Meaning: Ice

Divination Meanings: Obstruction, stasis, inertia, possibilities

Phonetic Equivalence: i (as pronounced in the word "indigo")

Pronunciation: ee-saw

Magic Usage: Inviting authority and power, stopping a phase or procedure

Water represents the fluidity in your life. It allows you to explore ideas. It encourages you to discover more. Ice, on the other hand, focuses on the solidity in your life.

This means that if drawn, Isa is a rune that is asking you to be more patient. It is similar to ice that will eventually thaw and turn to water.

However, unlike Nauthiz, Isa seeks patience for situations that have already occurred in your life.

This is because you could be experiencing a tense situation in a relationship, a blockage in your creative thought process, or even disagreement in your business dealings. These situations are temporary and fade away over time. So, you need to stay both determined and patient.

The rune reminds you not to resort to any rash action.

If you are expecting money in the present, there are chances that it might not come to you. As you wait for it to arrive, see if you can be productive. Learn new things. Experience new sensations. Chasing after money might only serve to delay its availability.

### *Reverse Isa*
This rune does not have a reversed position.

## *Jera*

⟨

Literal Meaning: Harvest

Divination Meanings: Development, progress, shifts, result

Phonetic Equivalence: y or j

Pronunciation: yare-awe

Magic Usage: Inviting long-term growth and success, bringing change, aiding with fertility

Harvest represents the idea of reaping what you sow. In essence, it communicates the idea of collecting the results of your hard work. The same principle applies to this rune.

When you draw this rune, it is an indication that you may be collecting the results of your hard work in the near future. However, it comes with a caveat; you must have sown seeds in the past. The greater the efforts placed, the more rewards you can collect.

As harvest season usually precedes a time of joy and celebration, the appearance of this rune takes place before a time of peace and happiness. Therefore, you may expect a fruitful time ahead.

This rune is concerned with the cycle of one year. This could mean one of two things:

1. You could expect something to happen in a year's time, or
2. You might be experiencing a period of good fortune, which may last for a year

If you are looking for new beginnings, this is a favorable rune to draw.

### *Reverse Jera*
This rune does not have a reversed position.

## *Eihwaz*

Literal Meaning: Yew Tree

Divination Meanings: Shelter, change, creation, empowerment, endurance

Phonetic Equivalence: ei

Pronunciation: eye-waaz

Magic Usage: Attaining spirituality, bringing about change, easing transitions in life

This rune has strong feminine symbolism. It portrays the personality of a powerful woman who is capable of bringing good or bad. This duality represents the dual aspects of change in life.

Changes are like a toss of a coin; the outcome may be favorable, or you may lose the toss. However, whether the change is good or bad, this rune predicts that the outcome might eventually benefit you.

The yew tree represented by this rune speaks of longevity. This is because yew trees regenerate from daughter trees that grow within them. As such, Eihwaz shows that you might enter a cycle of rebirth, where the new cycle may bring a fresh start to your life.

This rune also indicates movement. If you are involved in a business dealing or a form of expansion in your life – such as moving to a new home, expanding your business, or looking to add a new member to your family – this rune urges you to look to the future. These new additions may bring much prosperity into your life.

However, it is important to be flexible. To achieve your goals and dreams, you might have to adapt to new scenarios. So, do not hesitate to mold yourself to these situations.

### *Reverse Eihwaz*
This rune does not have a reversed position.

## *Pertho*

⌈

Literal Meaning: Lot cup or Vagina

Divination Meanings: Mystery, sexuality, fate, magic, prophecy, destiny

Phonetic Equivalence: p

Pronunciation: perth-row

Magic Usage: Assisting with childbirth, improving psychic abilities, aiding in divination and magic

This rune is difficult to decipher. While the most common meaning of Pertho is a lot cup - a type of box that was used for divination in ancient times - or vagina, there are other meanings attached to it, such as a chess piece, dice, hearth, and game.

What we do know is that this rune is about friendship, trust, and solidarity. It invokes warm feelings usually associated with being in the presence of a good friend.

You may discover friends from the past, helping you to relive fond memories.

This rune also speaks about knowledge and the idea that things are not always what they seem. So, if runecasters draw this rune first, they should put it aside so they can understand the other runes.

Pertho also emphasizes on inner transformation. It is an indication that things might not be the same again in your life.

### *Reverse Pertho*

This could mean disappointments due to having big expectations. You may experience these disappointments in the near future. Additionally, if you have done others favors, you may expect people to not appreciate or reciprocate them.

## *Algiz*

ᛉ

Literal Meaning: Protection or Elk

Divination Meanings: Shield, defense, sanctuary, and prayer

Phonetic Equivalence: x or z

Pronunciation: all-yeese

Magic Usage: Absorbing the protective energy of the cosmos, communicating with a divine force, asking for protection

This rune is a symbol of healing and protection, and you might find it used during meditational healings. It is also said to protect a person's family, friends, and close ones.

When you draw this rune, it means that you might face a challenging obstacle in the near future, but you may receive protection against its devastating effects.

You might find yourself receiving a boost in your career by your friend, particularly in the form of a new opportunity. If you find yourself interested in new things, this rune recommends that you explore these interests fully. There could be an opportunity waiting for you, possibly in the form of a business or career move.

Since this rune is an important symbol in meditational healing, drawing it is a sign that you might require introspection, mindfulness or healing in your life.

## *Reverse Algiz*

When the rune appears in reverse, it could indicate mental or physical health concerns.

If you have been overburdening yourself with other people's problems, it is now a good idea to take time for yourself. After all, if you are unable to function well, you will not be able to help anyone.

## *Sowulo*

ς

Literal Meaning: Sun

Divination Meanings: Success, energy, fertility, and popularity

Phonetic Equivalence: s

Pronunciation: so-woo-low

Magic Usage: Finding strength and vitality , and gaining enlightenment

This rune represents the love of a man for a woman. It also focuses on mental and physical health. If this rune is drawn by a man, he may expect love to enter his life in unexpected places. To a woman, this rune is an encouragement to show her love to the men in her life.

Sowulo indicates the presence of sound physical and mental health. You might enjoy a sudden recovery if you have been suffering a certain illness, or find your health protected against any harm. However, one should understand that the rune will not protect you from careless acts of endangerment.

You might discover the power to make changes in your life, whether for yourself or for others.

The sun is an indication of vitality. If you have been experiencing physical or mental fatigue, this rune may just give you the push you have been looking for.

## *Reverse Sowulo*

This rune does not have a reversed position.

# The Third ætt, or Tyr's Aett

This section will look at the aett of Tyz, or Tyr. It includes the runes Teiwaz, Berkana, Ehwaz, Mannaz, Laguz, Ingwaz, Othila, and Dagaz.

If you thought that Odin – and later Thor - were the only ones to enjoy the status of a principal godly being, you are in for a surprise. Some tales place Tyr as the leader of the Norse pantheon, before Odin supplanted him.

While Tyr was most notably known as a god of war, he was much more than that. His main duties were to uphold justice and the law. This gave him a much bigger status than originally imagined.

Also, Tuesday is named after Tyr (Tyr's day).

## *Teiwaz*

↑

Literal Meaning: Tyr

Divination Meanings: Victory, honor, justice, law, righteousness

Phonetic Equivalence: t

Pronunciation: tea-wahz

Magic Usage: Discovering spirituality, gaining magical equilibrium, healing wounds

When this rune presents itself, it is showing you the path of honor. It wants you to practice justice in your life.

This may be because you are involved in a conflict with someone or because you just witnessed something and are wondering what to do about it. Or, perhaps you know that someone has caused harm but is refusing to admit their mistake.

The rune suggests that it may be time for you to do the right thing. However, as this step might change the balance of things, you need to consider what results your actions might cause.

In its upright position, the rune is pointing "up", not in a literal sense, but in a symbolic direction. This direction refers to the heavens above, or Asgard. When Teiwaz appears in this position, the rune may grant you divine protection.

If you require answers to questions or guidance in your life, meditate with this rune in the upright position.

The symbol also represents an arrow tip and just like the arrow, be firm and true to your goals. If you are, new paths may open up for you.

### *Reverse Teiwaz*

If the Teiwaz appears in reverse, it might indicate the presence of a superficial relationship in your life. Whether a man or woman draws it, it requires more work from the individual to maintain the relationship.

The reverse position could also indicate problems with property, either in one you already own or in a property you might purchase in the near future.

## *Berkana*

ᛒ

Literal Meaning: Birch tree

Divination Meanings: Nourishment, fertility, beauty, healing, growth

Phonetic Equivalence: b

Pronunciation: bear-kawn-oh

Magic Usage: Gaining spiritual growth, receiving healing, finding sustenance

This rune sends spiritual vibes, and it is no surprise that if drawn, it suggests getting more in touch with the spiritual aspects of your life, not the materialistic ones.

You may want to take this time to pay more attention to your family and personal matters.

When the rune signifies personal matters, it refers to the act of experiencing the joys of life. Perhaps you could travel more. You could learn a new skill. You could try out a new hobby. Perhaps you could simply just connect with nature and take in its serenity.

The birch tree signifies a new beginning. This may occur in the form of a new baby, a new love interest, new business ventures, new career opportunities, or something else that is new, but valuable to you.

However, just like the birch tree, you must nurture the new gifts that you receive. If you do not take care of them, they might later exit your life.

### *Reverse Berkana*

In reverse, the rune might indicate the possibility of difficulties in growth. This lack of growth may be experienced in your personal or professional life.

If you feel that you are stuck in one spot, try to stop for a while. Take in your surroundings. Ground yourself and be present in the moment so you can figure out what to do next.

There may the occurrence of news that concerns the entire family. When such news appears, the key to facing this is to be supportive and understanding to your family members.

### *Ehwaz*

ᛗ

Literal Meaning: Horse

Divination Meanings: Travel, journeys, energy, communication, motion

Phonetic Equivalence: e (as pronounced in the word "ember")

Pronunciation: ay-wahz

Magic Usage: Succeeding in astral projections, aiding in transportation, assisting with communication

The horse is a symbol of travel and journeys. So, when this rune appears, expect to go on a journey soon. This voyage may be literal, where you travel and discover another country. Alternatively, it may be spiritual or emotional, where you begin a new experience to transform yourself. Either way, this rune indicates that it is a good time to start any type of journey.

When sitting on a horse, you have a better perspective of what is coming and what is behind you. In a similar manner, when you head out on your journey, you may find out your goals and what has been holding you back.

The rune may also denote a gradual development in your life, either in something you are already working on or a project in the near future.

### *Reverse Ehwaz*
This position might indicate problems in your

journey. This could mean that you may not get the opportunity to complete it.

There may be unexpected delays preventing you from going places or doing what you set out to do.

## *Mannaz*

ᛗ

Literal Meaning: Mankind

Divination Meanings: Community, family, relationships, intelligence

Phonetic Equivalence: m

Pronunciation: Mawn-nawz

Magic Usage: Representing a group of people, gaining transcendental awareness, establishing social harmony

Mannaz is a rune of shared experiences. The appearance of the rune reminds you to look at others in a new light. It wants you to avoid judging your fellow man with preconceived notions about race, gender, sexual orientation, color, and other factors.

It highlights that your view of others may be a reflection of your inner self. However, the rune reminds you that within everyone is the capacity to change and be more accepting. The presence of Mannaz indicates that now is the best time to connect with people. So, you may forge a strong relationship with an unexpected person.

If you are about to take a big step in your life, you may want to consult with someone first. Try to seek out expert's opinions and get feedback from people in your life. Try not to make decisions in haste.

With the presence of Mannaz, you might experience growth in your skill. This might come useful in your professional or personal sphere.

### *Reverse Mannaz*

This position might reveal the presence of enemies outside your culture. However, should you encounter your enemies, understand that they do not represent a group of people as a whole. So, Mannaz reminds you to approach each situation without connecting it to a bigger picture.

Legendary runemasters often mention that this position indicates the presence of a strict parent.

## *Laguz*

ᚱ

Literal Meaning: Water

Divination Meanings: Intuition, concern, counseling, and revelation

Phonetic Equivalence: I

Pronunciation: Law-gooze

Magic Usage: improving psychic abilities, revealing hidden things, and reducing emotional disorders

People attribute water to stillness and peace. When asked to imagine a body of water, people think about its calmer form, like a still lake, waves gently lapping at the beach, or a river stream peacefully flowing against rocks. However, water is also part of the ocean, and storms can capsize ships and swallow humans into its depths.

When this rune appears, it recommends you to take the time to think about your actions. Are they flowing gently like the river, or are they violent and dangerous, like a raging sea?

Being like a calm body of water may allow you to navigate obstacles with ease. On the other hand, being rash may destroy many aspects of your life. If you draw this rune, consider how you approach situations.

Just like how water brings life, this rune may indicate the arrival of something lively. It could be an object, a person, or an experience.

Water also cleanses things, so you may have to reflect on your inner self. Are you feeling calm and assured? Is there an inner turmoil threatening to disrupt your behavior?

These questions may lead you to undertake a spiritual cleansing.

### *Reverse Laguz*
If you spot this rune in reverse, it may indicate that you are being slightly aggressive or pushy. If you feel that you are assertive when dealing with situations, or, more importantly, with people, try to stop for a while. Try to take some time off to meditate or pursue rewarding activities. Then, return to the situation or person. You may then have a better approach to the situation or towards the person.

## *Ingwaz*

◇

Literal Meaning: Ing

Divination Meanings: Creativity, productivity, work, potency

Phonetic Equivalence: ng

Pronunciation: eeng-wahz

Magic Usage: Improving fertility, attaining orgasm, and reaching goals

Ing is the name of the God of agriculture and fertility. However, Ing is his Anglo-Saxon name. If you are familiar with Norse mythology, you might know him as Freyr.

This rune indicates a time of rest. If you have been working hard or dealing with a stressful situation, you may soon have time to relax.

It may also indicate the chance to tie up loose ends and the opportunity to find new beginnings.

Ingwaz also denotes strong sexual desire. With this rune revealing itself, expect a deep attraction with someone very soon. While many runecasters may explicitly mention that any attraction develops with the opposite sex, there is no restrictions or conditions on the gender you might get attracted to. You may have equal chances of developing attraction to either sex, depending on your preference.

This rune may also mean that a relationship could end - particularly one that has not been growing.

### *Reverse Ingwaz*
This rune does not have a reversed position.

## *Othila*

Literal Meaning: Property

Divination Meanings: Inheritance, ancestral property, home, land, enclosure

Phonetic Equivalence: o

Pronunciation: oath-awe-la

Magic Usage: Acquiring land, strengthening family bonds, gaining universal truth

Othila is the rune of inheritance. You may receive a literal inheritance: a home, property, assets, or even money. On the other side, you may inherit something spiritual, such as peace, attitude, confidence, or wisdom.

If you are venturing out on a spiritual journey, you may find that this rune is your best companion and may provide you with assistance.

You may receive something that you have been seeking for a long time in abundance. Keep your eyes open and your mind receptive to signs.

You may find yourself drawn to your home more often. This may be because your home is not merely a place of rest. It is where you are likely to find the most happiness, comfort, and peace. Try to maintain your home to the best of your capabilities so you can use it to find the strength to continue your journey.

### *Reverse Othila*

This might suggest damage on property or assets. You may also discover things missing or stolen. Be conscious of what you have on you. Try not to misplace or leave items in public places.

There might be disputes over inheritance but bear in mind that if you find dealing with them difficult, you may consider going home to regenerate.

## *Dagaz*

ᛞ

Literal Meaning: Day

Divination Meanings: Security, happiness, clarity, satisfaction

Phonetic Equivalence: d (pronounced as "th" in the word "these")

Pronunciation: though-gauze

Magic Usage: Reaching a higher level of consciousness, attracting positivity

If you have been stuck in a rut for a while, this rune may change that. As the sun breaks into a new dawn every day, you may find yourself in the process of finding clarity.

You may also have been in a dark place in your mind. Dagaz predicts that you may encounter light, as if you were exiting a long, dark tunnel.

The sun provides light and light is often a symbolic reference to a spark of inspiration. Therefore, after drawing this rune, ideas are more likely to flow through you. You may find your ambitions suddenly soaring to new heights. This is not a problem. In fact, it shows your thirst to accomplish many things. Try to keep your goals in perspective but your feet firmly on the ground. Your dreams may be bold, but your actions should be realistic.

If you have been concerned about your family, you may want to start taking steps to secure their future.

If you have been considering the idea of change, where you would like to try a new lifestyle or a new location, you may find that this is the opportunity to do so. However, keep yourself protected. Try to have backup plans in case you do not like the results of your change.

### *Reverse Dagaz*
This rune does not have a reversed position.

# *Chapter 4: The Art of the Runestave*

It is about time that we introduced a couple of terms here for you runecasters. As we will be using these terms often, it is a good idea to get used to them.

Runestaves: An object that has runes on it is called a runestave. We will speak about them in more depth as we continue our runic journey.

Vitki: Another name for a runecaster.

Lots: Refers to the runes. To keep it simple, we will mostly be using the word runes. However, if you do encounter this term, know that it simply means runes.

These terms not only bring out the essence of runecasting, but also put you in the right frame of mind to begin practicing your runic sessions.

So, get ready vitki, we are about to start!

# Creating a Runestave

One of the extraordinary aspects of runecasting is that it is flexible and can be done anywhere. If you are short on materials, you can simply write down the runes on slips of paper. The only rule is that you require 24 pieces of any object you choose to write on, one for each of the runes.

Traditionally, runes were painted on surfaces, typically using the color red. However, you can use a regular ballpoint pen to write the runes on your slips of paper.

However, I recommend you to create your own staves. There are numerous reasons for this:

1. Runes are powerful and you need to connect with your runes to use them effectively.

2. They are easy to create and, as mentioned above, you can begin practicing with objects you have at home.

3. As runes are magical, you need to add your energy to them, and that's why it is better to create runes rather than buy them from the market.

However, it is understandable if you would like to begin runecasting with some quality materials.

This will not just allow you to get used to working with the right objects but also make you feel that you have completed your vitki persona.

There are many types of runestaves available in the market, with pieces made of wood, plastic, wooden sticks, and even cards.

As runecasting is a personal journey, do not worry about getting a popular runestave. Experiment with different objects and see what feels comfortable.

If you are unsure if your runestave is comfortable, ask yourself the following questions:

1. Will I be carrying the runestaves with me or will I be carrying out all divination sessions at home?

2. How easily can I draw runes? Would I be better suited to using small pieces of wood or using cards?

3. If I am performing a runecasting for somebody, how comfortable am I using the tools that I have right now?

4. Which object will be easier for me to take care of and maintain?

There are other questions you can ask yourself to

get a "feel" of how you want to approach runecasting, but typically, you can start with the above.

Different runestaves fit certain types of castings. This is something you can think about when you improve your divination abilities. For now, know that you can use any runestave for most casting methods.

If you would still like to create your runestaves from scratch, try the method below. However, please proceed with caution - you will be working with sharp tools, so if you are unsure how to use them, please seek the help of a professional or someone experienced at working with wood.

History shows that runecasters use wood from birch trees, but you can select any tree to begin with. If you have a fruit-bearing tree in your locale, it is an ideal birch. If you are looking to make higher quality runes, you might have to look for yew and pine trees, However, you may begin with any tree.

Once you have selected the tree, approach the branch or piece of wood that you would like to cut. Try to look for a section that will give you a piece of wood that is at least half an inch in diameter. If the wood you get is too broad, you will have difficulty carrying it around. If it is too narrow, you might not be able to carve the runes into the wood.

Once you find the ideal section of the tree, collect 24 pieces to work with the 24 runes mentioned under the chapter, "Runes of the Elder Futhark."

Each piece of wood that you collect should be about 4 to 5 inches long. Using a knife, peel off the bark and smoothen the surface beneath it.

Another note of caution - working with wood is rather tricky. You will encounter debris and small pieces of wood that can get under your skin, and once they penetrate, they are difficult to pull out. Before starting, ensure that you use thick gloves and any kind of eye protection, such as glasses.

Once you have the pieces of wood, before carving the runes, we need to work on the rituals.

## The Hammer Rite

You should perform this rite if you are creating your own runes. When you are ready, begin by facing the North Star.

Start with the first rune, which would be Fehu. Create the sign using your fingers, with your hands extended in front of you. When creating the rune signs, your hands should be level with your face. When you create the rune, hum or say the name of the rune out loud.

When done, move on to the next rune and create it in the air, just like the first one. You should be able to create this rune slightly to the right of the first rune. This way, you should be able to create all 24 runes.

Do not worry if you are unable to find space to create the runes. You can start over anytime and give it another go. Do this until you have mastered the technique.

Next, return to the original position, facing the direction of the North Star.

You will now be creating the hammer sign. To do this, stretch your right hand out in front of you in a way that you can see your palm right in front of your face.

Now, move your hand downwards in the

direction shown below.

Stop your hand in front of your chest while keeping it stretched. From this position, you will need to make the shape of a bowl, moving your hand towards your left. You can see this movement in the direction indicated below.

When you complete the movement, your hand should be at the same level as your chest, but it should look like you are pointing slightly to your left. Next, you will have to move your hand from your left to your right, still keeping your palm at the same level as your chest. You can see this direction indicated below.

When you are done, turn 90 degrees to your right and perform the sign again. After finishing the sign in this direction, turn 90 degrees again and perform the sign for the third time. Finally, turn 90 degrees and do the sign again. You have now performed the signs towards the four directions symbolic in Norse mythology - North, East, West, and South.

Now that you know how to perform the hammer ritual, let's continue and move on to the next rite.

## Ritual of Formation

At this point, you should be ready (and perhaps excited) to carve the runes into the wood. To infuse your carvings with power, you should go through the right rituals. To help you get started, we will begin with the 'Ritual of Formation'.

Now, find a quiet place where you will not be easily disturbed. When ready, perform the Hammer Rite.

When you are ready, use a pencil to draw the rune lightly on the piece of wood. Do this with all the pieces of wood that you have with you, so you will have 24 pieces of wood with light pencil markings of the runes.

Pick any sharp object. A knife is ideal, but essentially, you just need something sharp to carve the runes effectively.

Each stave should have one rune. So, begin by picking out your first stave. As you are carving the rune, chant its name. Feel the vibrations of your chant flowing through your body as though they are stirrings of some hidden power.

The act of carving the rune into the wood equates to connecting with runic forces. It fills you with wisdom and clarity. Additionally, reciting the name of the rune helps you recollect its properties, names, uses, and other characteristics. So, carving is a spiritual process, but also an intellectual one.

For example, as you are carving the first rune, which is Fehu, and repeating its name, you will automatically recollect all its properties. This knowledge also adds strength to your carving.

Once you have finished carving the rune, you have to paint it. Ideally, most runecasters utilize red ochre. However, you can choose any form of red paint that is available to you.

Like in the process of carving, hum the name of the rune as you are painting it. You must do this process slowly and with steady hands so the paint falls into the grooves that you have carved.

After you have completed painting the runes, hold the stave in your hands and meditate on the properties of the rune. This will connect you with the rune and further strengthen your knowledge.

## The use of cards

When you have to lay down certain runic patterns, you might find that cards are convenient to use. There are many advantages to using cards. Here are a few of them:

1. Cards allow you to shuffle. This adds more chances of randomness and allows you to show the person in front of you that you are choosing a rune at random.

2. They are easier to carry around and fit inside your pockets or a small bag.

3. You can write down information on the cards. You can add the names of the runes, allowing you to quickly recall information. You can add in small symbols as references or make small notes. When you are making notes, write them in a way that only you would understand. The person receiving the reading should not be aware of the meanings.

4. Cards are ideal for beginners who would like to have a quick reminder whenever they are runecasting.

5. It is easy to make cards. You can purchase blank paper cards, which are not too expensive, and write your runes on them. If you have poster boards, you can use

those as well. You can also use regular paper. Now, let's show you how to make runes on paper using a few simple steps.

## Paper runes

To get started on your paper runes, you will need a few simple tools. You will need a word processor software on your computer or laptop, a printer, glue, and scissors.

### *Step 1*

Open your word processor and insert shapes into the document. Now, create a rectangle that you think would be the size of your card. I recommend a size of 2x3 inches.

It should look something like this (note that the dimensions below are an approximate representation and are not accurate):

If you feel like you need a bigger card, go ahead and change the dimensions.

Once you have created the rectangle, place your rune image on to it.

Now, add two more rectangles, but this time, fill them with black.

You will add these black rectangles behind your image card so that light does not filter through your card easily, allowing you to see your image card during the draw.

*Step 2*

Print out your designs on a regular A4 sized paper. Note that you do not have to use colors for the image card, and a greyscale image will suffice. Ideally, try not to use bold colors for the image. You can also try and adjust the transparency of the image so that it appears slightly "fainter".

*Step 3*

Using your scissors, cut out your designs. You should have three papers for each rune card you will be creating; one image rectangle paper and two black rectangle papers.

*Step 4*

Now, take your image paper and glue one dark paper behind it to create the first two layers of your card. Ensure that the dark section is facing outward. Now, you should be able to see your rune image on one side and if you flip your card, you should be able to see the solid black color.

On top of this solid color, glue the second piece of

black rectangle, once again ensuring that it is facing outwards. Again, you should be able to see the rune on one side and the black color on the other.

By adding two layers of solid color, you are preventing anyone, including yourself, from easily seeing the image on the card.

This should prove useful when you are runecasting and want to pick your cards randomly.

For the remaining runes, use the same steps as mentioned above, leaving you with 24 cards in total at the end.

Now, you have your first deck of runecasting cards. Congratulations vitki!

## Casting the runes

One of the items that you should keep with you is a white cloth. This white cloth can be made of any material, but it should be a surface on which you can easily place your runes. The idea behind this is that white symbolizes purity and impartiality. It also indicates the idea of a "blank slate", meaning that it does not hold any information or knowledge. This way, it does not affect or corrupt your reading. It is merely a surface to place your runes on.

Some runecasters choose to decorate their cloth. You can add some decoration too, as long as the designs do not hold any meaning for the reading. The design should be there purely for aesthetic reasons.

Typically, you should get the design stitched into the cloth. However, should you wish to paint, use black paint and keep the strokes as thin as possible.

## Containing the runes

When you are not using your runes, place them in a container. Most runecasters like using a simple pouch. The size of the pouch depends on the size of your runestaves. However, if you are holding cards, you cannot use a pouch.

In such cases, you can use a small packet or a box. If you want to get a box for your runes, there are numerous ones available in the market with unique designs and aesthetics.

## Theal's Stool

In advanced levels of runecasting, you will also need a three-legged stool, preferably made out of wood. While runecasting, you should sit on this stool. However, for most runecasting purposes, you do not need it.

## Understanding your Runes

Runecasting is personal. So, you can never attribute a set meaning to every rune for every scenario. It is up to you to draw meaning from them and invoke their knowledge. However, to become proficient at reading, you can commit to a few practices.

### *Practice 1*
Take out the runes of the first ætt and arrange them from left to right. Now, start from the first

rune, which is Fehu, and move your way towards Wunjo. As you shift from one rune to another, start making connections between the runes based on the runic knowledge you have gained so far.

For example, as you move from Fehu to Uruz, see what they represent together.

Here are a few questions that could help you achieve a level of understanding:

1. What does each rune mean?

2. What have I understood about Fehu?

3. What have I understood about Uruz?

4. If any of the runes were drawn, what does that indicate?

5. Now that they are connected, what do their connections represent? Is there a way for me to come to a sound conclusion by combining the meanings of these two runes?

These are some of the questions that arise when you combine runes. Of course, you may have plenty of questions you want answered. The trick is to not ignore them. You should not have doubts when you are in the middle of runecasting. So, it is better to discover the answer during the practice process.

Once you have reached Wunjo, try to do this practice in reverse. Start with the Wunjo rune and move back all the way to Fehu.

Repeat this as many times as possible until you are comfortable working with the runes.

After you have completed this practice with the first ætt, use the same practice on the second ætt. Start with Hagalaz and move all the way to Sowulo, then start going backward.

When you are confident with your understanding of the second ætt, move on to the third.

At this point, remember not to make more than two connections. You are only just beginning, so it is best to start with easy steps. Do not hesitate to refer to the information about each rune as many times as possible. You might often find yourself frustratingly trying to remember certain aspects. You might think, "What is wrong with me? I should know all of this!"

Try to take it easy on yourself, fellow vitki. You are only just beginning your journey. Keep in mind that the masters of history have gone through the same trials that you are experiencing, or might experience.

## *Practice 2*

In this practice, take the first rune from each ætt and arrange it from left to right in front of you.

You have Fehu on the left, followed by Hagalaz, and finally, Teiwaz on the right.

First, make connections between Fehu and Hagalaz. Refer to the information on the runes if you have to. Then, discover connections between Hagalaz and Teiwaz.

Once you have completed moving in one direction, go in reverse, starting from Teiwaz and ending on Fehu.

After you have finished working on the first set of runes, move on to the second set. Here, you will take the second runes from the first, second, and third ætts. Employ the same practice technique that you have used for the first set of runes.

Once you complete the second set, you can continue on to the third one. Keep practicing this way until you have completed eight sets (as there are eight runes in each ætt).

The main purpose of this exercise is to allow you to discover meanings between runes of different ætts.

### *Practice 3*

This is a more advanced level of practice. Here, you will pick two random runes and place them before you. Like in the previous practices, go through the process of finding meanings, connections, and relationships between the two runes. If you would like to get started, ask the questions established in Practice 1. As you go through the list, you will realize that you have questions of your own. As with Practice 1, do not brush them away. Try to answer each query that goes through your head.

Remember - you do not have to try every combination possible. The idea is to make yourself comfortable picking information about the runes in whatever arrangement they appear.

Think of Practice 3 as an exam; just try a few rounds and see if you are confident reading the runes. If you are, you can continue on to the next step.

## Meditate on the runes

With various meanings for each rune, you should consider contemplating all of them. Ideally, take a whole day for each rune. Look through all their meanings, including literal and divination meanings, its magical usages, its symbolism and see the knowledge that you gain in the process.

This practice is useful in gaining a deeper insight into each of the runes. It will help you form meanings that others may not know about. Each rune is multi-faceted; you can never consider one meaning to be the absolute and only meaning for each rune.

# *Chapter 5: Runecasting for Beginners*

After you have filled your cup of knowledge and honed your skills through the practice methods mentioned above, it is time to venture forth into your first runecasting.

Remember that there are no shortcuts to mastering the skill of reading. You essentially start with the knowledge, go through a few trials, then apply everything you know into actual practice.

However, you can start runecasting by yourself, as you will see in the first runecasting methods.

Always remember that every time you draw the rune, it should be placed face-down so you do not have a glimpse of the reading until the entire layout has been completed. Once you are ready to perform your reading, turn over the runes in the order that will be highlighted for each layout.

With that condition in mind, let's begin runecasting, my eager vitkis!

# One-Rune Layout

This is the most basic layout that you can use. This layout is ideal for beginners who would like to flex their runecasting abilities.

There are two ways to perform this layout.

1. You can cast the runes in front of you and pick one at random. With cards, you simply place them face down and make a random selection.

2. You can reach into your rune pouch to choose your rune. With your cards, choose one from the box or packet you have placed your cards in. If you do not have a container of any sort, simply shuffle your cards and pick one at random.

Think about your questions first, then draw the rune in front of you. Align the rune properly so that it is not lying sideways or diagonally. Make sure you do not look at the rune without aligning it properly, as runes should be in an upright and reversed position. You should not willingly change the outcome of your reading.

You must understand that as this is a simple cast, so you cannot imagine complex questions. This draw is most suited for yes or no questions.

Place the chosen rune in front of you, as shown

below.

Rune 1: When you are ready, turn the rune around. Try to see if you can gain more understanding from its position in relation to your question. The answer might be a simple yes or no. Overall, this spread gives you a general attitude or a broad feeling towards your question. If you are starting out with this layout, you could also record the session for future reference.

## *Recording each session*

You may not always gain the best insight the first time around, especially when you are a beginner. In order to learn from past runecastings or find out if you have made mistakes, try to record your sessions on a piece of paper. You do not need to have a complex system of notes. All you need are the following sections:

Date:

Question asked:

Rune drawn:

Initial readings formed:

Additional notes:

You will find that by writing down your session, you will get a better understanding of it, often coming up with clearer interpretations of the rune. Furthermore, when you refer back to your sessions, you can make additional notes. In turn, this will help you perfect your art.

## Two-Rune Layout

This layout focuses on the aspect of duality. Instead of thinking of time as the past, present, and future, this layout imagines time as "what is" and "what will become".

As always, think of the question in your mind. Here, your query does not have to be a question that requires a yes or no answer.

Draw two runes, like how you did for the One-Rune layout.

They will be arranged in the following way:

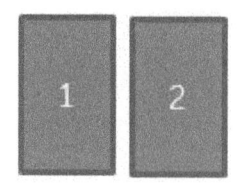

Rune 1: "What is." When you are looking at this rune, your first approach is to think of how it answers your question in relation to the past. Then, ask yourself what is happening in the present. How has the past influenced the situation you are in now?

Rune 2: "What will become." Finally, focus on what it says about your future. Does it tell you how events will play out? Does it talk about the future in general?

### *Recording the Session*

As with the One-Rune Layout, you can record your session for future insights or learning. For the Two-Rune Layout, the following are the questions that you might require:

Date:

Question asked:

Runes drawn:

Initial readings formed from Rune 1:

Initial readings formed from Rune 2:

Additional notes:

# Three-Rune Layout

The concept of the Two-Rune layout might seem alien to many. We understand time in three concepts; the past, the present, and the future. The idea of "what is" and "what will become" might take a while to get used to. If you feel that the Two-Run layout does not fit your divination technique, you can move on to the Three-Rune Layout.

This layout not only focuses on the three common ideas of time but also gives you a deeper understanding of your question.

Think of the question in your mind. As your question will be more complicated than the one used during the Two Rune Layout, take time to give it focus and clarity. When you are ready, draw the runes.

Begin by drawing your first rune, which represents your past. Place this rune on the cloth or surface in front of you.

Next, draw the second rune, representing your present, and place it to the right of the first rune.

Finally, draw the third rune, representing the future, and place this to the right of the second rune.

As always, make sure that the runes are face-down. As time moves from the past to the present, and then to the future, we draw the runes in the same pattern. This gives you a more accurate reading as well, as it shows that you went with the flow of time, instead of jumping to a specific point. Look at the picture below to see how the runes should be placed.

When you are ready, turn the runes over.

Rune 1: Shows how the card affects your past. It could be telling you a story, or it could be giving you a straight answer.

Rune 2: Gives you an insight into the present by talking about your present situation.

Rune 3: It gives you an idea of the future and shows you what might happen.

### *Recording the Session*
For the Three-Rune Layout, here are the sections for your notes:
Date:

Question asked:

Runes drawn:

Initial readings formed from Rune 1 - Past:

Initial readings formed from Rune 2 - Present:

Initial readings formed from Rune 3 – Future:

Additional notes:

## Four Directions Layout

Norse mythology treats dwarves in a rather unique manner. Most works of fiction have given us the idea that dwarves hide in mountains and smelt molten iron into weapons for war. They drink a lot of mead and are generally crass.
Not according to the Norse. In their mythology, four dwarves actually hold up the sky in the four directions we use today.
Austri holds the sky up in the east.

Vestri holds the sky up in the west.

Nordri holds the sky up in the north.

Finally, Sudri holds the sky up in the south.

So, the dwarves were generally depicted as strong beings.

For this layout, we shall be following this representation of the four directions. Let's begin.

As always, think of your question. This current layout can support questions that are more complicated, so take your time to focus on your query.

Once you are ready, draw four runes.

Place the first rune towards the top of the cloth or surface in front of you. This rune indicates the north.

The second rune will go below the first rune, but slightly to the left. This rune indicates the west.

The third rune should go below the first rune, but it must be in line with the second rune. This is the east position.

The final rune will go below the second and third runes but will stay in line with the first rune, indicating the south position.

Here is how the layout should look:

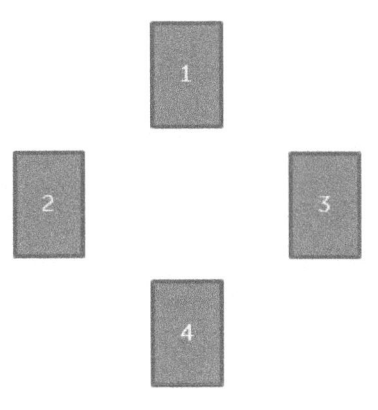

When you are ready, turn the runes over.

Rune 1 – North (Nordri): Represents what influences have occurred in the past, depending on the question you have asked.

Rune 2 – West (Vestri): Represents the present. Everything that is happening and influencing your life based on the question you have asked.

Rune 3 – East (Austri): Represents the future. The possible outcomes, based on the rune you have drawn.

Rune 4 – South (Sudri): What do you understand from the entire layout collectively? If you put the information from Nordri, Vestri, and Austri together, what are the runes trying to tell you?

## *Recording the Session*

For this layout, the sections you should record for your sessions are the following:

Date:

Question asked:

Runes drawn:

Initial readings formed from Rune 1 - Nordri:

Initial readings formed from Rune 2 - Vestri:

Initial readings formed from Rune 3 – Austri:

Initial readings formed from Rune 4 based on the previous three runes – Sudri:

Additional notes:

# Five-Rune Layout

In this layout, we will be invoking the power of the elements to give us the answers to our questions. Norse mythology includes five elemental forces - earth, air, fire, water, and spirit.
The presence of these elements gives us a deeper understanding of our question and even shows subtle insights into our life, situation, and future.
Start by imagining your question.
When you are ready, pick out the first rune and place it on the cloth or surface, preferably towards the center. This rune represents the spirit element and just like its position, it indicates that your spirit should be centered at all times.

Next, pick your second rune and place it to the left of Rune 1. This is the position of the fire element.

Choose the third rune and place it above Rune 1, in the position of the earth element.

Select the fourth rune and place it below Rune 1, in the position of the water element.

Finally, select the fifth rune and place it to the right of Rune 1. This position represents the air element.

The layout should look something like this:

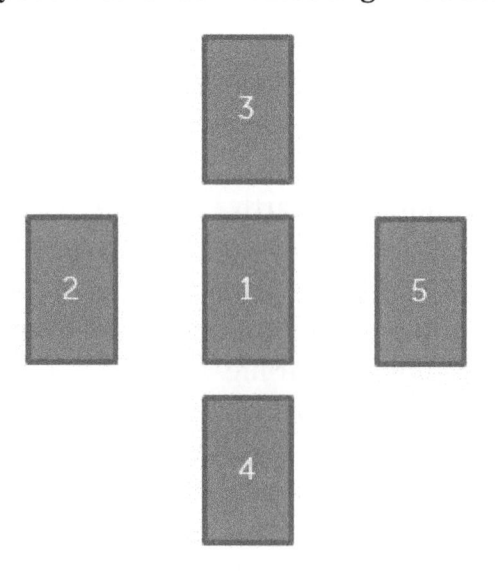

Rune 1 (Spirit): This rune represents your present situation. It might reveal to you the problem the way it is now. Also, look at this rune to find out your current spiritual status. Are you lacking in spirituality or are your feelings strongly connected to your spirit?

Rune 2 (Fire): A rune in this position is talking about the past. What has occurred in the past to bring you to your current position and how does it influence you? Fire is the symbol of raging emotions, so look to this rune to understand your emotions. How do you feel about the events in your past?

Rune 3 (Earth): This is the position that reflects if you might get any help to deal with the problem at hand. However, if you draw a negative rune, it does not always mean that you will not receive any help. It could also indicate the fact that you are finding it difficult to accept the results of this layout. In this layout, earth symbolizes the body, so use this rune to find out about your health and see if there is anything to be worried about.

Rune 4 (Water): This position informs you of the parts of the problem that are outside your influence. So, you may or may not be able to affect their outcome. A rune in the upright position may also signify a lack of obstacles whereas a rune in reverse may show the presence of many of them. If you draw a rune without a reverse meaning, it is assumed to be in the upright position.

Rune 5 (Air): This rune represents the future. It speaks of the outcome in the future and is also the cumulative reading of all the runes that have been picked so far. This rune is the conclusion to this layout. The attachment to the air element denotes the intellectual aspect of this rune. It could highlight whether you will have the mental fortitude to face what is coming, or if you will be burdened by stress.

### *Recording the Session*

For this layout, the sections you will require for your notes are:

Date:

Question asked:

Runes drawn:

Initial readings formed from Rune 1 - Spirit:

Initial readings formed from Rune 2 - Fire:

Initial readings formed from Rune 3 – Earth:

Initial readings formed from Rune 4 – Water:

Initial readings formed from Rune 5, based on the previous four runes – Air:

Additional notes:

## The Persona

This is a simple 5 spread layout that you can use

to hone your runecasting skills even further. It keeps the balance of a single-row layout but exercises the complexity of using five runes.

To start with this layout, imagine the question in your mind.

Pull out the first rune and place it towards the left side of the cloth. Take out the second rune and then place it to the right of the first rune. Follow this with the third, fourth and fifth rune, each placed to the right of the previous one.

In the end, you will have a layout that looks like this:

Rune 1: This rune highlights where you are right now in your life. Think about how the problem or question currently affects you.

Rune 2: Use this rune to discover the main thoughts and concerns that are in your mind. These are the thoughts and concerns that trouble you the most in relation to the question. When you look within yourself, you might sometimes find that there are numerous thoughts swirling in your mind. Do not be alarmed. Focus on the question and you may find out which thought you need to pay attention to.

Rune 3: This rune is used to find out your heart's deepest desire right now.

Rune 4: Use this rune to find out the primary focus in your life right now. What are you aiming for? Where do you want your life to be? If the rune appears in reverse, it may indicate that you are spending too much time dwelling on the negatives.

Rune 5: The last rune gives you insights into your future actions. It may also present you with changes that might occur in the future and what these changes might mean to you.

### *Recording the Session*
The following are the sections you can use when recording this layout.
Date:
Question asked:

Runes drawn:

Initial readings formed from Rune 1:

Initial readings formed from Rune 2:

Initial readings formed from Rune 3:

Initial readings formed from Rune 4:

Initial readings formed from Rune 5, based on the previous four runes:

Additional notes:

# Runic Cross

This layout combines elements of the Five Rune Layout and The Persona. This rune will help you gain a bigger picture of your situation, and goes in more depth than the previous layouts on this list.
Start by imagining your question or problem. Since this layout uses more runes, take the time to truly understand the question that you would like to ask.

Once you are ready, begin with the following steps.

First, place the first rune close to the center of the cloth. Leave more space below the first rune, as you will be adding two more runes below it.

Take your second rune and place it to the left of Rune 1.

Your third rune goes above Rune 1.

The fourth rune goes below Rune 1.

The fifth rune goes below Rune 4.

Finally, Rune 6 falls to the right of Rune 1.

With the layout complete, it should look like the image below.

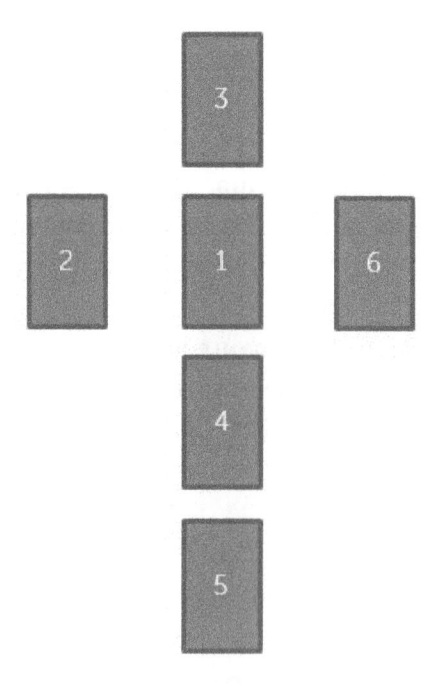

Rune 1: We start with this rune which represents all the opportunities that you have right now. You can use this rune to see if you might get help in the near future, and how much help you may receive.

Rune 2: This is the rune of the past. It is used to reveal all the actions that led to the situation you are facing in the present. It may also speak about your role in the situation if you were directly involved.

Rune 3: In this layout, Rune 3 represents the most probable outcome. Use this to hone in on what you can expect to happen next.

Rune 4: This is the rune of the present. It reflects the current situation, and you may also use this to think about what you are feeling. Did the previous three runes help you deal with the current situation better, or did they predict that you will be putting in more efforts to deal with the situation?

Rune 5: This rune helps you understand all the influences that are affecting your questions. Is your question affected by your family, friends, emotions, status in life, or any other factors? This is the first layout that asks you to reflect on the very nature of your question.

Rune 6: Finally, Rune 6 is the rune of the future. You might notice that you have already discovered a rune that shows the most probable outcome. However, while you have a probable outcome, the rune for the future may let you know how much effect the outcome has on your future. Will there be more challenges ahead? Or will you find help in the most unexpected places?

***Recording the Session***
In this layout, the following are the sections that you can record:

Date:

Question asked:

Runes drawn:

Initial readings formed from Rune 1:

Initial readings formed from Rune 2:

Most probable outcome formed from Rune 3:

Initial readings formed from Rune 4:

Initial readings formed from Rune 5:

Initial readings formed from Rune 6, based on previous runes and to answer if you can affect or change the outcome of Rune 3:

Additional notes:

# The Mirror
This arrangement is specifically made to answer questions about your professional life or your

career. You may use this layout to ask about business decisions, career moves, or investment choices. The choice is yours.

As always, begin focusing your attention on the question you have in mind. Try to keep it strictly business related. Let's look at an example. You may not ask questions such as, "how will my business affect my marriage?". Rather, it should be along the lines of "should I make a career move in the immediate future?"

Of course, your question may have much more complexity than this, but it should strictly focus on business, career, and your professional life.

If you are wondering why this layout is given the name "mirror", it is because it represents a traditional mirror with a handle.

Begin by focusing on your question.

Now, draw six runes and place them face down in front of you.

Place the first rune near the bottom of the cloth.

The second rune goes above the first rune.

Place the third rune above Rune 2.

Place the next two runes below the third one. However, place one slightly to the left and the other slightly to the right of Rune 3.

Starting from the bottom and moving up, you now have four rows of runes. Rune 1 on the first row, Rune 2 on the second, Rune 3 on the third, and Rune 4 and 5 on the fifth.

Place the final rune above Rune 4 and 5 in a way that it aligns with the first three runes.

Your arrangement should look something like this:

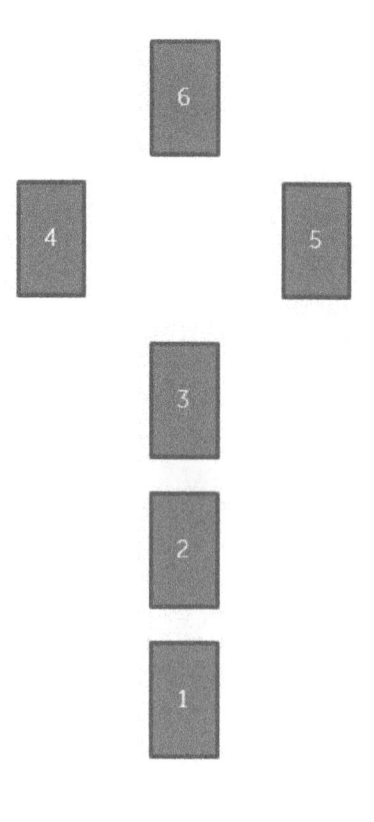

Now that the arrangement is complete, let's start reading the runes.

Rune 1 – This rune speaks about your past. With this rune, you may find out whether the past had any bearings on your current situation.

Rune 2 – This is the challenge position. Use this to know if you are currently facing any challenges in regards to your question or problem.

Rune 3 – The third rune symbolizes strength. Use this rune to find out qualities about yourself that make you strong, especially in regards to your question. These qualities will help you solve the problem at hand. In this position, if a rune lands in reverse, do not focus on its reverse meanings. At this point, you are only trying to find out your strengths based on the qualities of the rune.

Rune 4 – This rune represents your present scenario and what you are currently facing.

Rune 5 – Using this rune, find out your perception of the future. Sometimes, you may be trying to put on a brave façade, but there might be feelings of apprehension or worry lurking beneath the surface. Use this rune to discover those feelings so you can come to terms with them. Of course, an upright rune shows that you may not have any negative perceptions about the future. In that case, move on to the last rune.

Rune 6 – The final rune is used to discover the future. This is your final outcome. If your rune lands in the upright position, you may be rewarded in the future. If it lands in the inverse position, your future may not look welcoming. However, regardless of the position of this rune, you still can change the future depending on what you discovered in the previous runes.

For example, let's assume that the sixth rune landed in a reverse position. It might indicate a few troubles in the future. However, the third rune shows your strengths and the fifth rune may indicate a positive perception about the future. By combining the features of these two, you might just have the tools ready to take on any situation in the future.

The power is within you, vitki!

### *Recording the Session*
In this layout, you can record the following sections:
Date:

Question asked:

Runes drawn:

Initial readings formed from Rune 1:

Initial readings formed from Rune 2:

Initial strengths discovered from Rune 3:

Initial readings formed from Rune 4:

Initial readings formed from Rune 5:

Initial readings formed from Rune 6:

Initial readings formed from Rune 7:

Additional notes:

## The Seven Rune Layout

As this layout uses seven runes, at this point, you may get more details about the nature of your question, its past influences, and how your future looks like.

Use this layout to ask questions that cannot be answered quickly. While you may ask a yes or no question, it is far better to seek broader answers. The following are a few examples for your inspiration:

How will my relationship progress if I continue down my current path?

Will I find happiness if I choose to stay in my

current job role?

When there are no easy answers to these questions, this rune might help you find the clarity that you require.

Let's now begin.

Think about your question and meditate on it for a couple of minutes.

Once done, take out seven runes.

Essentially, you will be placing the first six runes in a row. So arrange Rune 1 through 6 in one row, where Rune 1 is the furthest to the left and Rune 6 is the furthest to the right.

Below the first row of six runes, place your seventh rune in a way that it remains in a central position when compared to row number one.

Here is how the arrangement should look:

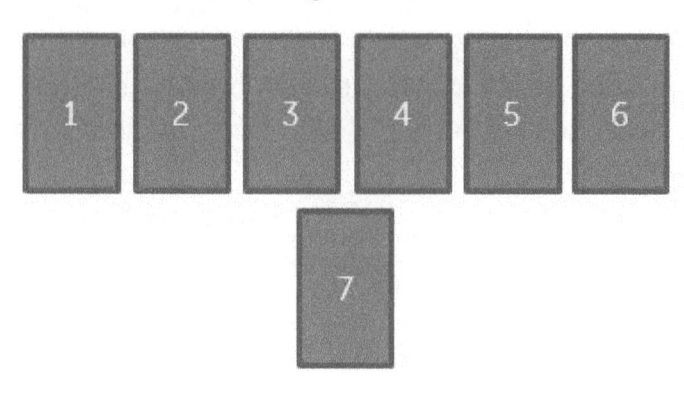

In this reading, you will be focusing on two runes at the same time, before moving on to the seventh and final rune. So, whenever you're ready, flip the runes.

Rune 1 and 2 – These runes represent the nature of the problem itself. They may give you insight into how the problem affects various parts of your life.

Runes 3 and 4 – Use these runes to understand the past and how it has affected problems in the present.

Runes 5 and 6 – These are two powerful runes and quite possibly the most essential ones in the layout. Use these two runes to get advice and recommendations, taking extra care to form meanings in relation to each other. These runes do not speak of the future, but rather how to tackle the problem, how to create opportunities for yourself, and how soon you should act on this advice. Even if you draw runes in reverse, do not worry; reverse positions are also recommendations, explaining what you are doing wrong, and how to rectify your stance in regards to the problem.

Rune 7 – Unlike other runes in this list so far, this does not predict the future, but rather the outcome of your readings. Whether this rune generates a positive outcome or a negative one, the end result will depend on the previous runes.

For example, Rune 7 might appear in reverse. However, that may not indicate a negative outcome because Rune 5 and Rune 6 gave you strong recommendations to deal with the problem. These suggestions may balance out the reverse position, or perhaps even negate its effects.

Use this and the coming layouts to prepare for the more advanced layouts that you will encounter.

### *Recording the Session*
The following are the sections you can use to record this layout.
Date:

Question asked:

Runes drawn:

Initial readings formed from Rune 1 and 2:

Initial readings formed from Rune and 4:

Initial readings formed from Rune 5 and 6:

Initial readings formed from Rune 7:

Additional notes:

# Mimir's Head

Finally, we move on to the final layout in our beginner's section. While we understand that you are excited to try this layout, remember that it is best to practice with the previous layouts before reaching this point. This layout is slightly unique, so the best way to explain its arrangement is by using rows, where each row will feature the arrangement of the runes in a particular order.

When you complete the layout, you will notice that it has a diamond shape.

Let's assume that there are five rows in front of you.

Row 1: This begins at the very top, towards the center of the layout. Here, you will place Rune 7.

Row 2: Here, you will place Rune 6 and Rune 8, where Rune 6 is positioned slightly to the left of Rune 7, and Rune 8 slightly to the right of Rune 6.

Row 3: Here, we will be placing the next couple of runes in relation to the positions of Rune 6 and Rune 8. Rune 5 will be placed to the left of Rune

6 and Rune 1 will go to the right of Rune 8.

Row 4: In this row, we will be placing the next two runes using the same alignment as Rune 6 and Rune 8. Rune 4 will be placed in the same vertical alignment as Rune 6 and Rune 2 will be placed in the same vertical alignment as Rune 8.

Row 5: In the final row, we shall place Rune 3 in the same vertical alignment as Rune 7.

When you have completed the arrangement, here is what the layout should look like:

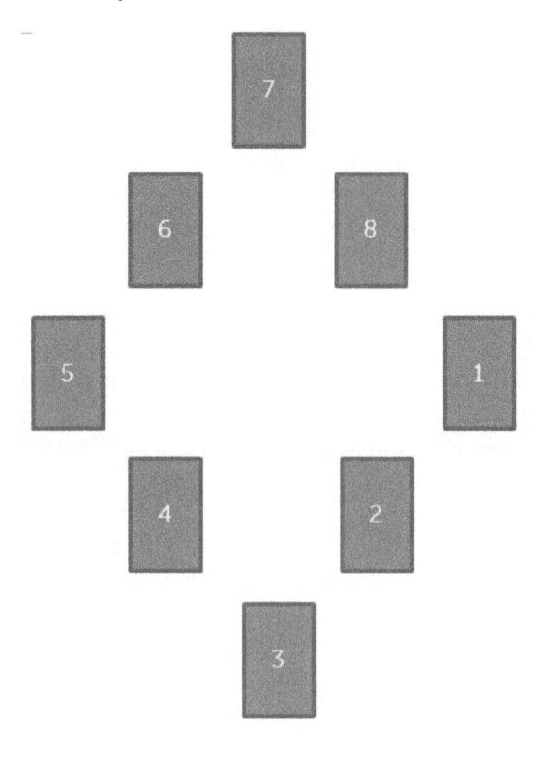

Whenever you are ready, let's move on to the reading of the layout.

Before you start, note that each of the positions represents our common understanding of directions; north, northeast, east, southeast, south, southwest, west, and finally, northwest. Each of these directions are ruled by a particular rune, which is not the rune that you draw. When you begin your reading, focus on the relation between the rune that you have drawn and the rune that rules the direction.

Let me show you an example.

The position of Rune 1 is east. In this layout, Berkana governs the position of the east. However, Berkana is not the rune that you will draw. It is the rune that gives meaning to the position. Let's assume that you drew Thurisaz for the position of Rune 1. So, you should focus on the relationship between Thurisaz and Berkana to discover meaning from the runes.

If you draw a rune that corresponds to the governing rune, the effects are double. If you draw a rune that is in opposition to the governing rune, the effects get negated.

Example: Using the same example as above, let's

assume that you drew Berkana as Rune 1. As Rune 1 is already governed by Berkana, you double the effects of your reading. If you draw a rune that has the opposite meaning of Berkana, you may not gain any further reading from the position. They cancel each other out.

Now that we have established the rules, let's get down to the actual reading. Begin turning over the runes in the order established below.

Rune 1 (East): Direction of Berkana. Focuses on the beginning of your problems. Provides better insight into questions related to birth and motherhood.

Rune 2 (Southeast): Direction of Laguz. Focuses on the growth of your problem. Shows you how to increase your energy. Talks about initiation, or if something new is about to start in your life.

Rune 3 (South): Direction of Dagaz. Speaks about sudden changes that may appear.

Rune 4 (Southwest): Direction of Thurisaz. This position focuses on defensive powers. Gives you insight into what protection you may receive from enemies, outside influences, or threats.

Rune 5 (West): Direction of Kenaz. This position focuses on giving you inspiration. Look for signs of ideas or recommendations hidden among the meanings you derive from this position.

Rune 6 (Northwest): Direction of Hagalaz. This position talks about transformation. In other words, based on your question, look at how you or your life might be transformed.

Rune 7 (North): Direction of Jera. Here, you can discover what rewards you may receive now or in the near future. Look for signs of success, positive developments, or a sense of completion.

Rune 8 (Northeast): Direction of Algiz. From this position, you can find sources of strength. Let it speak to you about how you can find courage, power, or the morale boost you have been looking for.

One of the changes you will notice about this layout is that there is no rune to discover a final outcome, unlike some of the other other layouts before. This is because as you move in a clockwise direction from one rune to another, you will begin to gain more clarity about your question. It is like finding different pieces of a puzzle and then slowly putting them together. When you are done, the final picture might tell you all you need to know about the outcome of your question.

However, this layout requires a lot of practice before you can begin to easily derive meanings from its arrangement. You may find yourself referring to rune meanings frequently. As this is a more complex layout, you might expect to encounter a few failed readings as you slowly gain mastery over it.

### *Recording the Session*
To record this layout, you can include the following sections:
Question asked:

Runes drawn:

Initial readings formed from Rune 1 based on the direction of Berkana:

Initial readings formed from Rune 2 based on the direction of Laguz:

Initial readings formed from Rune 3 based on the direction of Dagaz:

Initial readings formed from Rune 4 based on the direction of Thurisaz:

Initial readings formed from Rune 5 based on the direction of Kenaz:

Initial readings formed from Rune 6 based on the direction of Hagalaz:

Initial readings formed from Rune 7 based on the

direction of Jera:

Initial readings formed from Rune 8 based on the direction of Algiz:

Additional notes:

## Beginner's Tips

Are you still with us on this journey? Good. There is still so much to learn and discover. You are only on the tip of the iceberg; from here on out, you will discover a ton of abilities that are hidden beneath the surface.

The techniques mentioned in the "Runecasting for Beginners" section are arranged in increasing order of complexity. First, you have the easiest form of divination, the One-Rune Layout. Following this, each layout gets more challenging in order to flex your runecasting skills and improve your knowledge before you begin to work on the more advanced techniques.

However, it is time to bring your attention to a few points.

1. Take your time with each layout. Try to familiarize yourself well with each one before moving on to the next. Being

proficient in one layout allows you to approach the next one with relative ease. Each layout will offer a different type of challenge and will require varying degrees of patience. You may master the One-Rune Layout within a week or so. However, it might take you a long time to be comfortable with the next technique. Eventually, when you reach the more complex arrangements, you may have to spend at least a month acclimating yourself to its routines. That's okay. This is how it is meant to be practiced. Master runecasters have dedicated years to fully control their divination capabilities, and they still find many secrets to unearth.

2. While practicing the layouts, patience is required. Also, you should meditate whenever possible. The art of meditation opens up your mind and frees you from the fog of thoughts you may have. Having a clear frame of mind grants you with better patience, which in turn helps you learn faster. If you find yourself frustrated, or easily losing focus, take some time out to pay attention to yourself. Deal with the things that are troubling you; meditate if you would like to, or simply take a short walk.

3. Do not force yourself to discover meanings. Let them come to you. Use the knowledge you have about the runes to derive meanings. When in doubt, refer to the information about the runes. While it is good to be eager to know more about the runes, know that their meanings will only come to you through repeated practice.

4. No rune will give you a fixed answer for a specific question. Your intentions, experiences, the past, and the present are just some of the factors that come into play. To derive the greatest meaning, be honest with yourself.

5. You will only be using the session notes for the beginner techniques. This is to help you refer to your notes and better understand your approach. You may be able to spot mistakes, discover another way to approach a problem, find more solutions or meanings, and even figure out how to better align the runes. The advanced techniques are complex and your readings cannot easily be put into notes.

6. You might notice that when you are arranging the runes, the instructions may not always ask you to arrange them in

order, from Rune 1 to the last rune. In such cases, do not worry about the order. It is not the order of arrangement that matters, but the order in which you turn the runes over once you have completed the arrangement. Keep this rule in mind as you work on the advanced techniques as well.

7. Once you have mastered the beginner's techniques, you may want to test your skills on others. During this time, it is also recommended that you learn at least the first advanced technique so that you are well equipped to deal with almost any question or problem presented to you.

With the above points in mind, let's now move on to the more advanced techniques of runic divination.

# *Chapter 6: Advanced Runecasting Techniques*

Are you ready to become a master runecaster? If so, here are some advanced techniques for you. Remember that a lot of these techniques might be confusing to grasp, but it will be easier to understand if you have firm control over the beginner's layouts that were shown in the previous chapter.

As you go through the advanced techniques, note that you may have to spend more time focusing on your question. Typically, you should spend at least a couple of minutes or more pondering your question or problem. During the thinking phase, shuffle the runes if you have them in your hands, or move them around if they are held in a box, pouch, or any other container. These advanced layouts provide complex answers. For that reason, some of them might be confusing to you if you jump straight to the layout without preparing your question.

## The Four Quarters

We will begin with The Four Quarters, an arrangement named after the four quarters in a year. It is ideal to give you accurate answers about your question.

As the layout focuses on the concept of a year, it gives you an insight into the life you had led for the past six months, and using that information, gives you knowledge about the next six months.

Start by meditating on your question while shuffling the runes. Allow your question to pick the runes. When you feel like it is time to pick, select eleven runes and arrange them in front of you.

You do not have to draw the runes quickly. You can take as much time as possible between each draw. Allow your question to guide you.

Now that the runes are displayed in front of you, arrange them in three rows. Each row will have three sections; left, center, and right.

Let's start with the top row first.

## *Top row spread*
Left: Rune 2
Center: Rune 3 and Rune 4
Right: Rune 5

## *Middle Row Spread*
Left: Rune 1
Center: Rune 11
Right: Rune 6

## **Bottom Row Spread**
Left: Rune 10
Center: Rune 9 and Rune 8
Right: Rune 7

You will notice that the arrangement moves clockwise, starting at Rune 1 and ending at Rune 10, with Rune 11 in the center of the arrangement.

The layout should look something like this.

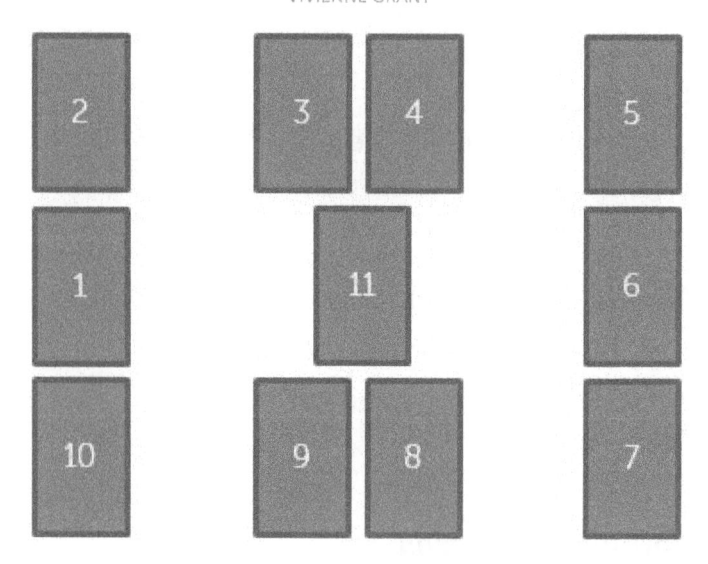

With the arrangement complete, let's now move on to the reading.

Rune 2, Rune 1, and Rune 10: These three runes represent the first quarter of the year. They represent the situation in the present. They also give you insights into your current state of mind.

Rune 5, Rune 6, and Rune 7: These three runes are attributed to the second quarter of the year. They show you whether you may be receiving assistance, or whether you may face opposition when it comes to your question.

Rune 3 and Rune 4: These two runes on the top represent the third quarter of the year. You can think of them as warnings or advice, depending on how the runes turn out for you. They reveal to you what may happen if things continue on the same course as they are now.

Rune 8 and Rune 9: The bottom two runes represent the fourth quarter of the year. These runes tell you what is likely to happen in six months.

Rune 11: The final rune is an amalgamation of your readings. It is the conclusion of your journey, starting from the first quarter of the year and ending at the fourth or last quarter. You can use this rune to give you additional information and clarity or to provide a conclusion to your readings.

# The Tree of Life

In Norse mythology, we only know of one tree - Yggdrasil. This layout is representative of that tree, which is the center of the cosmos. The great tree knows all and extends its branches into the farthest reaches of the universe.

This layout is a representation of that knowledge. Just like the tree, you will receive a comprehensive reading from this layout. It will provide you with an overview of your life, or that of another person if you are doing the reading for someone else, and it will allow you to examine life from a different perspective.

Let's now borrow knowledge from the great tree and embark on a quest into the cosmos of our life, where we hope to find answers to some of the more elusive questions we have.

Before you start your reading, remember that you should start your divination differently if you are doing it for someone else.

If you are doing the reading for yourself, begin by meditating on your question. Shuffle, mix or move the runes around while you are thinking about your question. If you are doing the reading for someone else, let them mix the runes themselves. Ask the person to think about the question while they are mixing the runes.

When you or the other person is ready, draw ten runes. Remember that during the drawing stage, it does not matter if you are doing the reading for yourself or for someone else; as the runecaster, you should always be the one to pick the runes.

There is a reason for this; the person with the question has to shuffle the runes because they have to connect with the great tree of Yggdrasil. The tree will then absorb the question and provide the answer in return. However, the answer can only be understood by the runecaster as they have a link to the tree's great knowledge. For this reason, the runecaster picks out the runes and arranges them out for the divination process.

Now, let's arrange the runes out in front of us.

Begin by placing Rune 1 near the top of the cloth or surface.

Below that, place Rune 3.

Next, place Rune 2 to the right of Rune 3.

Rune 5 goes next, which you will place below Rune 3.

Then, take Rune 4 and place it to the right of Rune 5 and below Rune 2.

Then, pick Rune 6 and place it below Rune 5

Rune 8 will then go next, landing below Rune 6.

Follow this with Rune 7, which will be to the right of Rune 8.

Rune 9 gets its turn next, falling just below Rune 8.

Finally, place Rune 10 below Rune 9.

Once you have completed the arrangement, your layout should look something like this:

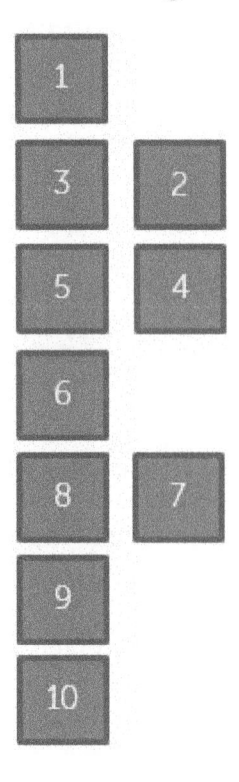

Rune 1: This rune represents your beliefs and how you view yourself. It may also reveal your level of confidence.

Rune 2 and Rune 3: You should read these two runes as a pair. Rune 2 represents your vitality. It may speak to you about your energy levels. Rune 3 is focused on your mental and physical well-being. Together, you can determine how you are feeling right now, both physically and mentally. Are you experiencing mental or physical exhaustion? Do you feel no motivation in many aspects of your life? Do you think you are physically weak and unable to continue on the journey of life?

Rune 4 and Rune 5: Rune 4 looks at your ethical and moral constitutions. It is the way you view the world, society, people, nature, and other aspects. Rune 5 centers on your recent successes. At first glance, it might seem like Rune 5 does not have any connection to Rune 4. However, when you combine their results together, you might start noticing meanings. Here are a few examples to guide you:

Do you feel that your recent successes were morally acceptable? Did you have to sacrifice someone else's well-being in order to gain what you wanted? After you had achieved victories, did you share your gains with someone, or, perhaps, use your victory to assist someone?

Rune 6: This rune represents your health. While Rune 3 focuses on the levels of energy you have physically, Rune 6 speaks about your health and if you are suffering any illnesses.

Rune 7 and Rune 8: With Rune 7, you may explore insights about your relationships and love. These could be issues regarding trust, new love discovered, lack of communication in your relationship, and other related knowledge. Rune 8 focuses on the arts and whether or not you have a creative endeavor in your life. When you combine the two runes together, it talks about how your romantic life and relationships are affecting your ability to seek out activities that boost your creativity and give you a sense of joy or to engage in a hobby.

Rune 9: This rune represents your creativity and your levels of imagination and whether or not you are able to utilize them in your personal or work life.

Rune 10: Home is where you set your roots, and this rune denotes your standard conditions of living, the situation of your home and how comfortable you feel in it, as well as other related knowledge.

## The Cosmos

Now, let's venture forth into the cosmos itself. The universe is a mystery. It is an enigmatic darkness that hides the answers to the big questions. Astronomers and physicists are still trying to unravel its origins (the most popular theory being the Big Bang) and, with much vigor, discover how the universe will end.

But when the universe presents its answers, it is not a simple answer where we can just simply nod and say, "I see". It is more like a great bang that makes us go, "Wow! I did not expect that".

Through this layout, we are looking to the universe to discover that big bang (no pun intended).

In this layout, we are asking the great tree to reach into three worlds in the Norse mythological cosmos; Asgard, Midgard, and Utgard.

Follow the same steps you have been following in the advanced techniques layout. Meditate upon the question while you shuffle the runes. When you are ready, pick out eleven runes.

As there are multiple layers to this arrangement, we will set down the runes in rows. In total, there are five rows of runes.

Row 1: Rune 10, Rune 9, and Rune 11 are placed on the first row, with Rune 9 in the middle, and Rune 10 and 11 on the left and right of Rune 9, respectively.

Row 2: Place Rune 8 below Rune 9.

Row 3: Now, arrange Rune 5, Rune 6, and Rune 7

in the same way as Rune 10, Rune 9, and Rune 11. Rune 6 will be in the center, below Rune 8. Rune 5 and Rune 7 should fall to the left and right of Rune 6 respectively.

Row 4: Place Rune 4 beneath Rune 5.

Row 5: Rune 2, Rune 1, and Rune 3 are arranged similarly to Row 3, where Rune 1 is in the center, and Rune 2 and Rune 3 are placed to the left and right of Rune 2 respectively.

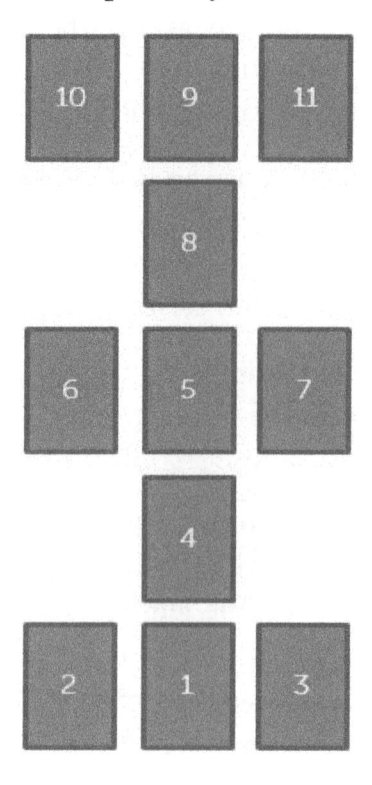

Now, let's dive into the three worlds for their

wisdom.

Rune 1: This rune refers to a major influence you have had in the past. It could be a person, an event, an object, or even a location.

Rune 2: This rune show you how you feel about this influence. You should look to your subconscious to find out more about your feelings. Do you feel that it was unfair that things happened to you? Do you blame someone for the situation? Do you have feelings of guilt, perhaps because of something you might have done?

Rune 3: This rune shows how you have been reacting to this influence. These are the most obvious reactions you have been displaying, such as joy, anger, disgust, sadness, envy, or any other reaction.

Rune 4: This rune represents the effects those influences have caused the situation in the present.

Rune 5: The fifth rune denotes your overall condition in the present. For example, have you suffered trauma and is that trauma still affecting you? Have you found ways to recover from the influences in your life?

Rune 6: You may use this rune to discover your current feelings or unconscious reactions.

Rune 7: This rune focuses on your conscious reactions.

Rune 8: This will show you what will happen if you do not change the trajectory of your life. If you do not handle the problem, you may just find out the effects that decision might have on your life.

Rune 9: You may use this find to find out the major outcome that may arise in the future based on your question or problem.

Rune 10: Once again, you will examine your feelings towards the outcome predicted by Rune 9.

Rune 11: Examine your explicit and outward reaction to the outcome predicted by Rune 9.

Note: This is the first layout that actually delves deeper into your reactions towards the outcome predicted by the runes. It allows you to examine your thoughts and feelings, and see if you can change them to eventually alter the outcome. For example, if the rune mentioned troubles in your professional life, try to examine how you feel and react to that. If you have been feeling unconfident, perhaps you may be able to set a new course in your professional life by changing that part of yourself. By being more positive and confident, you may eventually face the outcome of Rune 9 and discover better job opportunities, business prospects, financial solutions, and more.

## Celtic Knight Cross

The deeper you get into the advanced runes and their layouts, the more accurate you get in your runecasting. In this layout, one of the main differences is the presence of a rune known as the Significator.

This rune is a special rune that you have a personal connection with, or that you feel fits your life, personality, or fits you as a person. So how exactly do you find this rune?

Well, since this rune will play a vital role in this layout, let's select it first.

There are two ways to choose this rune.

1. Place all the runes face-up on the cloth or on the surface in front of you. Get a feel for the runes. Understand each one. Allow their meanings to flow through you. When you are ready, find out which rune you find yourself drawn towards, or which you have the greatest affinity for. If you are doing the reading for another person, simply ask the individual to pick a rune for you. Even if the person in front of you does not have all the knowledge of the runes, simply ask them to look at each rune to pick one that connects with them.

2. Another method is to simply choose a rune

from memory that you feel reflects you. At this point, you might have a thorough understanding of the runes. Pick one you feel gives the most meaning to your life. If you are performing the reading for someone else, we recommend the first option, where you ask them to choose a rune that connects with them. However, if you know the person well, you may pick a rune for them.

3. If you feel that the first two methods don't work, try this one instead. Think about the question in your mind. If you are doing the reading for someone else, reflect on their question. Once you have understood the nature of the question, pick a rune that represents it. For example, if the question pertains to home, property, or strong family ties, you may pick Othila. If the question focuses on sexual desires, you may choose Ingwaz.

Once you have chosen the Significator, place it on the cloth or on the surface in front of you.

Arrange the next set of runes in the following way:

Place Rune 2 to the right of Rune 1.

Place Rune 3 to the right of Rune 2.

Place Rune 4 below Rune 2.

Rune 5 goes to the left of Rune 1.

Place Rune 6 above Rune 2.

Rune 7 goes to the right of Rune 3.

Next, place Rune 9 to the right of Rune 7.

Rune 8 goes above Rune 9.

Rune 10 falls below Rune 9.

Place Rune 11 below Rune 10.

Finally, place Rune 12 to the right of Rune 11.

Once you have accomplished the above, your arrangement should look something like this:

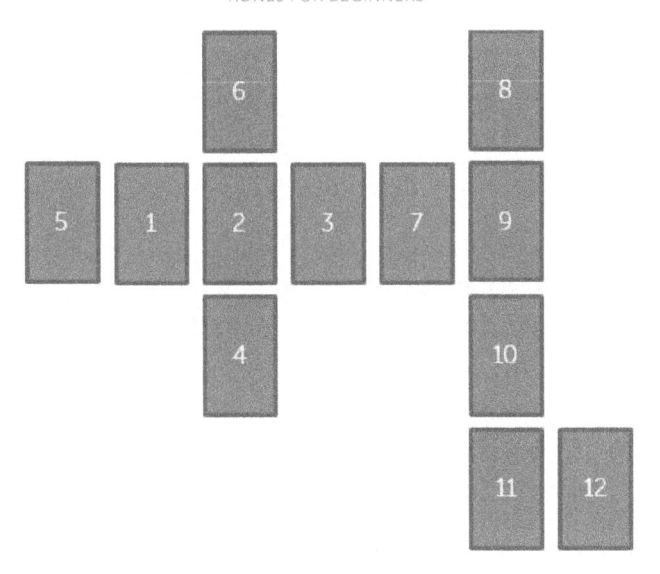

Now, it's time for the reading.

Rune 1: This is the Significator. It represents either you or the person who is getting the reading done. You can use this rune to find out more about yourself or the person getting the reading.

Rune 2: Use this rune to understand the nature of the question itself.

Rune 3: Here, you can find out any influences you might have in the future, whether they are positive or negative.

Rune 4: This rune represents the things from the past that have deeply affected you. This may include your childhood as well.

Rune 5: This rune speaks about departures. You might have a person, object, personality trait, or other factor leaving your life right now. Find out what it is.

Rune 6: Here, you will reflect on the various factors that will either guide you or be a threat to you in the future. This rune also depends on Rune 3 and Rune 4 as they help derive deeper meanings and help you reveal the idea behind the rune in much clarity.

Rune 7: This rune shows you the factors in the future that may greatly influence your life. These could be your parents, your partner, an object with sentimental value, or anything or anyone else of importance.

Rune 8 and Rune 9: You must read these two runes as a pair. Rune 8 represents your hopes, while Rune 9 indicates your fears. By gathering your hopes and fears together, you will understand how you stand in relation to the question. Sometimes, your hopes and fears may be the same thing. For example, you may hope to find a new job, but that can also be something you fear. Perhaps you may be fearful of giving up what you have. Or, you could be worried about change.

Rune 10: Family, friends, and relatives play an

important role in this rune. You may understand if you will be receiving support from them, and who amongst them might be the best person to approach if you require assistance.

Rune 11 and Rune 12: Here, two runes are used because they provide you with two options to proceed forward. You may receive two positive solutions. You may also receive two negative solutions, or it may be a combination of the two. However, do not discount a negative solution simply because it has a negative connotation to it. For example, one of the runes might suggest that you should look for love in your life, while the other may recommend you to wait. Obviously, we all know what may be perceived as a negative rune. However, the answer might not be simple. So, it is up to you to decide how the solution fits your life.

# The Futhark

Now, we have reached one of the most detailed runic readings, but because it is comprehensive, it requires a lot more practice with the runes before you can use this layout in your sessions. This layout stands out because it uses all 24 runes. At this point, the rune is typically used to predict the outcome for the next year.

Therefore, this is one of the most popular reading methods used just before the New Year.

This layout requires a lot more time to read. With all 24 runes at work, you will have to ensure that you take the time to read each one in a specific manner and in relation to another rune.

Whether you are performing this reading for yourself or for someone else, you have to ensure that you spend at least five minutes meditating on the question and mixing the runes. If you are doing the reading for yourself, you will have to meditate and pick the runes. However, if you are doing the reading for someone else, allow the person to meditate while you mix the runes.

When you are ready, place the runes by order of arrangement of their respective ætt's. For this, you will have three columns with eight runes in each column. Column 1 lies on the left, Column 2 lies in the middle, while Column 3 is on the right.

## *Column 1*

Arrange the runes of the first ætt one below the other, with Fehu at the top of the column and Wunjo at the bottom.

## *Column 2*

Arrange the runes of the second ætt one below the other, with Hagalaz at the top of the column and Sowilo at the bottom.

## *Column 3*

Arrange the runes of the third ætt one below the other, with Tiwaz at the top of the column and Othila at the bottom.

Your arrangement should look something like this:

When you have completed the arrangement, it is time to move on to the reading.

Rune 1: Fehu. How will you receive money or wealth? Use the rune to find out about sources of money, people who might help you gain more wealth, and other questions related to money.

Rune 2: Uruz. This rune focuses on your physical well-being and health. Your well-being could be related to the levels of energy you have, whether you are experiencing tremendous stress, if you are getting enough sleep, and so on. Health-related topics cover illnesses, deficiencies, injuries, and other questions.

Rune 3: Thurisaz. Are you going to face any opposition? This could either be a person or a physical impact, such as injuries or physical attacks.

Rune 4: Ansuz. Find out about your creative expressions. Discover whether you will get the right spark of imagination at work or in your project.

Rune 5: Raidho. Let this rune speak to you about travels. Will you be going on a journey across the globe? Will you be experiencing spiritual journeys through transformative techniques?

Rune 6: Kenaz. Allow this rune to guide you in your sexual relationships. Will you discover someone who will bring the right amount of sexual pleasure into your life?

Rune 7: Gebo. This rune will talk about something that will be given to you. It could aid you or cause harm.

Rune 8: Wunjo. Find out more about your relationships with this rune. Friends, family, loved ones, and acquaintances will make their appearance in this rune's predictions.

Rune 9: Hagalaz. Here, you will discover transformation. Who or what may cause transformation in your life?

Rune 10: Nauthiz. Find out what you desire, but are not successful in obtaining. This object of your needs could be the source of your restlessness.

Rune 11: Isa. Perceive what is holding you back. It could be an emotion, a person, or even a location.

Rune 12: Jera. The rune of rewards. Find out the results of your hard work.

Rune 13: Eihwaz. Discover the obstacles you will be facing. Find out about any hidden influences.

Rune 14: Perhtro. How will you find happiness in your life? Also, will you discover skills that may be beneficial to you?

Rune 15. Algiz. You may find out about a factor in your life that will require a lot of attention.

Rune 16: Sowilo. You may know if there is

someone or something there to guide you in the future.

Rune 17: Tiwaz. You may receive knowledge about assistance or insights into legal matters that you may be facing. These legal matters may already be ongoing or are likely to appear in the future.

Rune 18: Berkano. You may have the knowledge to understand what will help you grow and create beauty in your life.

Rune 19: Ehwaz. You may find out what relationships might become part of your life. These may be work, family, or sexual relationships.

Rune 20: Mannaz. You may gain insight into your overall mental health. You may also connect with your spiritual self.

Rune 21: Laguz. Here, your state of emotional balance comes into question. How will you be able to tackle the problems that may arise in the future?

Rune 22: Ingwaz. With this rune, you may find out two aspects. The first aspect concerns a factor that you spend a lot of time pondering. This may be your family, job, relationship, or wealth. The second aspect may be your sexual expression and identity, and the form it may take.

Rune 23: Dagaz. You might be able to discover what brings balance into your life.

Rune 24: Othila. Many predictions may occur through this rune. You may find out about the source of knowledge in your life. You may gain insight into family matters that you have been meaning to consider. You may find out about your political affiliations. Additionally, you might also receive insight into social concerns; will you be helping the community? Should you spend time for a social cause? Or, it could be something as small as your immediate locale, where you could provide assistance in a number of ways.

Note: Once you have done your readings, it is important to note them down so that you can refer to them over the course of the year. As these predictions could occur at any time during the year, you may want to return to them for reference.

## The Airts Method

We move on from one complex layout to another. In the beginner's section, we learned about Mimir's Head, a form of runecasting method that utilized the idea of eight directions in physical space. The Airts method utilizes the same concept. It is a blend of Mimir's Head and The Futhark.

Here, the eight directions will be inscribed on a wheel. However, each of the ætts will be represented on a different wheel. With this, the complexity of the reading intensifies.

Unlike the Futhark, however, each of the ætts gives you a different form of reading.

As we go through the layout, we will understand each wheel, and what each airt in the layout means.

Let's see what the wheel represents.

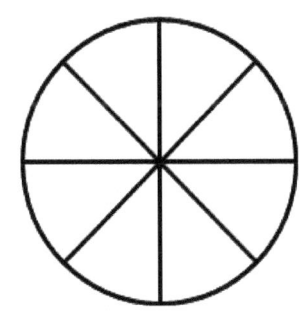

When you look at the wheel, you should be wondering where the north is. In the above wheel diagram, the directions do not fall into the wheel, but around it, and they are represented by the lines.

Taking this into account, we can notice that the line pointing straight up is North, with the Northeast on its right. Then comes the line pointing to the right, indicating East, and so on until we reach Northwest.

When these directions divide the plane into eight parts, each part is called "ættir", "airt", or "eights" in common English.

Each of the eight divisions gives space to a particular rune. Since we will be filling 24 runes into the airt, for this purpose, we will be using 3 airts.

Therefore, the first airt will be Freya's ætt.

### *Freya's ætt: Discovering insights into everyday matters*

Begin by drawing the first rune of Freya's ætt into the top right section. Then, move clockwise, placing a rune into each space until you have filled up all the spaces with runes.

Once you have drawn or painted the runes, you can begin to draw the runes you have.

Draw runes randomly and place them next to the painted or sketched runes in each space of the wheel.

Now that all of the runes have been placed, you can begin your reading. The spaces represent what meaning you should derive from the rune and based on their type, the runes themselves will give you meaning.

For example, let's assume that you have drawn Mannaz and placed it in Fehu's spot. The space for Fehu represents the idea of discovering financial benefits or wealth in the future. However, one of the insights Mannaz gives you is about community, family, and relationships. So, your reading may include the following questions:

Will my family help me if I fall into any financial trouble?

Can I depend on my friends to gain financial strength and stability?

Of course, the questions should be unique to you and should represent what you are seeking in the runes.

It is always advised to take the time to perform this reading. Some runecasters are known to take days to fully finish the readings. Once the reading is done, you should note down the results so that you may refer to them anytime in the future.

With that in mind, let's proceed to understand what each space means.

Fehu: Discovering financial strength and wealth in the near future.

Uruz: Represents your health, whether positive or negative.

Thurisaz: Focuses on aggressive conflicts with friends, family, business partners, and other people in your life.

Ansuz: The various communications in your life. Are you able to freely express yourself, or communicate with the people in your life?

Raidho: It tells you if things in your life are heading in the right direction or not. Perhaps you are waiting to make a decision.

Gebo: If you have made a contract, this rune may let you know if this contract will affect you positively or negatively.

Wunjo: You might discover the things you wish for, or they might not be available to you.

Now, we move on to the next wheel.

## *Heimdall's ætt: Discovering answers regarding psychological matters*

For this wheel, we will create a separate wheel and draw the runes of the second ætt into it. Hence, we will begin in the top right space again by drawing the Hagalaz rune. As we move clockwise, we continue drawing the other runes of the second ætt until finally, we finish with the Sowulo rune.

Once we have the runes on the surface, it is time to draw our runes.

Meditate upon the runes as you draw them. Pick the runes at random and place them next to the painted runes in the space. Your wheel should now look similar to this diagram.

Once you have placed all the runes, as you did with the first airt, read them in connection with the painted rune.

The following is what each of the painted runes signifies.

Hagalaz: Speaks to you about your unconscious psyche and what its condition is at the moment.

Nauthiz: Describes the strength of negative forces in your mind such as anger, shame, guilt, and others.

Isa: Mentions the effects of thoughts or feelings that you may not be willing to let go the future.

Jera: If you might receive any hope in the future and if possible, where you might receive it from.

Eihwaz: The strength of the motivational forces in your mind. Also, it might mention if your sense of purpose improves in the future.

Perthro: If the creative part of your mind will grow, diminish or stagnate over time.

Algiz: How well your mind might protect you from outside forces and external threat.

Sowulo: Your position in your mind or, in other words, if your self-esteem might become better or worse.

Once you have completed the reading for the second airt, let's move on to the last airt.

### *Tyr's ætt: Discovering insights into relationship matters*

You can think of this airt as a bridge between the first two airts. The first airt focused on external patterns and predictions. The second aett focused on your inner world. The third airt is a combination of the two previous forms of prediction.

With this airt, you will be paying attention to the relationships in your life. They could be with your family, your coworkers, your business partners, your sexual relations, your friends, or other people in your life. By focusing on the external aspects of these relationships along with your inner self, we might be able to gain a better knowledge of how well you fit with other people.

The following are what each of the runes tells you:

Tiwaz: Gives you insights about your creative energies and how these energies affect your work, projects, and tasks. Here, your sense of justice is brought to light. It may also predict whether your leadership qualities are good or need improvement.

Berkano: Brings into focus fertility and may indicate the presence of a baby in the future. Also, it may inform you of the strength of your family bonds. If you are a female, you may expect answers to maternity and if you might need any help with it.

Ehwaz: How well you adapt in your relationships,

whether you cooperate and work well with others, and how you view joint efforts in a relationship.

Mannaz: Gives you an idea of how you may view people at large. Shows you insight on your prejudices so that you may work on them to better yourself. Shows you other people's attitude towards you and if they might improve over time. Also, it indicates if you might have more friends or enemies in the future and brings into focus your intellect.

Laguz: Describes the stability of your emotions. Shows the level of imagination you possess and how well you may be utilizing it in your work. Also, it mentions affections received from others and if you may receive more of them in the future.

Ingwaz: Describes how expectations play out in your life, and whether they might be satisfied, or if you might receive any disappointments.

Dagaz: Describes balance. Whether you may have more light in your life (joy, happiness, love, sexual freedom), or whether you may be under the influence of a burdening shadow (despair, loss, constriction, regrets). New beginnings are also mentioned here, and whether you may easily transition into a new life, location, or personality.

Othala: Speaks to you about your home and whether you are comfortable in it or not. It highlights your relationship with your country, and in turn, the pride you may feel for your heritage. Also, it shows you if you may have opportunities to establish your foundation in another location entirely, whether it is another town, city or country.

## Worldstead Layout

The final layout we will be looking at for advanced divination methods is the worldstead layout. Here, you will notice that numerous concepts from Norse mythology blend into one rather complex layout. By combining different aspects and symbols, you are practically drawing power from various sources to discover the meanings of your predictions.

However, with the presence of a lot of variables, the complexity of this method is extreme, so you will have to be well-versed in the knowledge of the runes and be able to discover many of their meanings. You should have meditated about the runes and know more about them than through the information that is readily available to you. Every runecaster goes through the phase of deeply understanding their runes. We discussed the process of meditating upon your runes, and how to go about it. However, to be able to easily use this layout, you might not require just one day of contemplation. Often, you might find meanings to your runes through everyday experiences. Perhaps you might be visiting the park and the interactions between parents and children might spark your imagination. So, when thinking about it deeply, this insight might give you a better meaning about the runes. Whatever method you use to discover meaning, you must understand that learning is a continuous process. So, you could learn something from practically any source. You might discover something while solving a math problem, for example. Or, something might strike your consciousness as you are reading a scientific paper. The opportunities are endless. The only thing holding you back is you.

We also recommend a period of meditation. Mindfulness is a great way to center yourself and remove any blockages that might be interrupting a free flow of thoughts. You should not only meditate when you feel like your readings are not proceeding smoothly, but also at any opportunity you receive.

You must have fluency in every technique that we discovered so far and be able to use any of the techniques to match the situation, the person, the question, or the complexity of the problem.

Throughout history, runecasters have spent an enormous amount of time mastering the Worldstead layout.

Of course, if you wish, you can begin practicing it. However, bear in mind that if at any point you find yourself unable to grasp information or make connections, you should stop the process to study the practice with the previous methods, or study the runes.

The Worldstead Method is a figure that shows a two-dimensional representation of multidimensional space. Here, you will notice that the nine worlds of Norse mythology are brought together on a flat surface.

Therefore, it is important for you to have this design with you. If you will be constantly traveling with your runes, perhaps consider placing the design on a piece of cloth. Alternatively, if you are practicing runecasting inside your home or in other indoor areas, you may want to create the layout on a table or on other similar surfaces. Whatever method you choose, ensure that you draw them as accurately as possible, keeping in mind the lines and spaces.

Let's first get to know this layout well before we

begin casting upon it.

Runes or lots that fall into the inner sections of this layout are indicative of the conscious and subconscious status of the person, their feelings and emotions, as well as their frame of mind. The inner sections consist of the central circle, featuring Midgard, and the outer circle divided into four sections for Asgard, Svartalfheim, Hel, and Lyosalfheim. The spaces of Svartalfheim and Ljosalfheim focus on personal identity, which is directly linked with the person's psychological aspect. The regions of Asgard and Hel go beyond the limits of personal identity and may include altered states of consciousness.

Any runes falling into the outer regions of Nilfheim, Jotunheim, Muspelheim, and Vanaheim are focused on how the external forces affect the person.

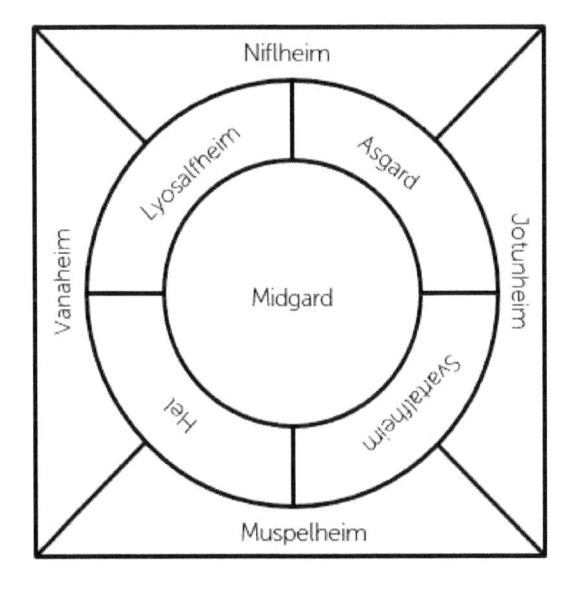

With this layout, you will be casting the runes blindly on the cloth or surface. There is no specific arrangement for the runes and there are no specific patterns to follow. Every draw is unique because one does not know where the runes will fall. They will be read based on the regions that they fall into.

If you cast the runes and notice that some of them fall face-down, you have two options to deal with them:

1. You may remove them from the cloth entirely

2. You may treat them as though they were inverted.

This decision has to be made before the casting and once you have decided on your course of action, you cannot change it after drawing the lots.

If you spot inverted runes, they cannot be considered inverted and should be read as if they were placed in the upright position. If you notice any runes outside the boundaries of the diagram, you may disregard them entirely.

Do note that there is no fixed number of runes inside the diagram. Every draw is unique and tells a personal story. So, you must be prepared to spot even just one rune within the diagram.

When you are ready, throw your runes on the diagram and begin your reading. Many times, the final picture may be too complex to understand in just one single session. For this reason, it is recommended to record your sessions. Draw the space and the location of each rune as it fell on the diagram. You should also draw the way the runes appeared, whether facedown, upright, or inverted. Runes that fell outside the diagram should also be indicated.

There are many ways to perform the reading. You may start from the innermost circle of Midgard and then move your way outwards or you may choose to begin at the outer sections and move inwards to discuss the personal matters at hand. The choice is entirely up to you. It is recommended to experiment with both ways and see which feels right or comfortable for you. You need to be able to do the reading easily and draw out the complete picture. This requires not only practice but a level of ease that you need to develop with the diagram.

Let's look at what each region or space on the diagram represents.

Midgard: How different people affect your life. It shows the way you interact with these people and if your interactions are positive or negative. It reveals the outcome in life pertaining to your question. Here, how the question affects your personality is brought into the light.

Asgard: Your connection with a higher presence. You may find out about your connection with divine entities and the cosmos. You can use this space to find out different aspects of your question. The space also focuses on matters of integrity and the fairness you show to fellow human beings. Here, you can find out about your sense of individuality and if you have the freedom to be the person you want to be. You can also see how the question relates to your spirituality, should you wish to do so. For example, do you feel the need to connect with your spiritual self?

Do you feel at peace? You can find the answers using this section.

Svartalfheim: The impact of creative influences in your life and work. Aspects of money. Things in your life that you may need to pay more attention to. How you can take charge of your life using what you have to place yourself in a better position.

Hel: Desires that you may be suppressing within you. Any negative influences from the past that may be affecting your life right now. Finding out the hidden meaning of the question.

Ljosalfheim: Influences on your mind and subconscious. Matters concerning your family. The possible directions that you may take in your life.

Niflheim: Things which resist you or that may be difficult to obtain. You may find out about various external restrictive forces that seem to prevent you from achieving a goal, communicating with a person, or even guiding your life forward. You may discover things in your life that might be lying dormant. In Norse mythology, Nilfheim refers to the "fog world". The fog is symbolic of mental blockages and other harmful effects from the subconscious mind affecting your consciousness. Fog may also represent the stirrings of conflicts, either with yourself or with others.

Jotunheim: Aspects of your life that cause confusion within you. Things that you have no control over or can't influence. The parts in your life that require change. Any crisis that you may face in the future.

Muspellheim: Discover energies that vitalize you, external influences that affect you actively or frequently, and aspects of your life that require movement.

Vanaheim: Encourages growth in your life. Gives you clarity on erotic or sexual relationships, or situations regarding people of the opposite sex. Allows you to discover more well-being in your life, as well as if anything in your life might change drastically in the near future.

Here are a few techniques that you can use to make effective castings with this layout.

Cast all twenty-four runes on your casting cloth. There are two approaches to casting.

1. You may elect to simply turn your rune bag upside down and give it a sharp shake before you toss the runes towards the casting cloth. This method works well.

2. Alternatively, if you feel confident about it, you may reach in and grasp all twenty-four runes in your hand before you then toss them gently into the air above the cloth.

As the runes land and settle on your cloth, you will form an instant impression. Did the runes land in a pattern or are they chaotically spread?

Are they all collected towards a certain point of the cloth? This would indicate a dominant field of the reading. For example, if most of your runes fall into the region of Nilfheim, your reading will be based on that region. Or is it widely dispersed? This would mean your reading will be based on multiple regions.

Are certain runes more prominent in your first view? Whatever your initial thoughts are, hold these in mind as they are invaluable at shaping your reading of the runes. It is essential to remember that this instinctive reading is free of all conscious interference.

Runes that are close together are deemed to be directly influencing each other. So, if Hagalaz and Fehu are touching, for example, you should focus on discovering their meanings as pairs. Remember that many runes may fall close to each other. However, to perform a pair reading, the runes have to be touching each other. The readings of runes that are isolated have their own individual meanings, with very little influence on other runes.

Here is another tip to help you with your divination process:

When casting the runes for divination, it is recommended to lay a cloth on the surface that you intend to cast on. The thicker the cloth, the more it will cushion the arrival of the runes. If you cast the runes onto a hard surface, it may result in the runes bouncing and rolling away from you. Avoid chasing runes across a room as it breaks the mental link with the act of divination.

With that, you are now a master at learning to work with the runes.

# *Chapter 7: Discovering more about the runes*

## Meditating With the Runes

Earlier, I mentioned runic meditation, and you might be wondering how to approach it in the best way possible. Fortunately, I can assist you with that.

When you perform meditation with the runes, it is not only an opportunity to gain more wisdom about the runes themselves but also to connect yourself to their source of magic. When you begin to develop personal connections with the runes, you will be able to invoke their meanings and power easily. This makes your transition into a master runecaster easier.

After you make connections with the runes, you are practically opening the gates of your mind to receive their understanding.

However, you should know that you do not have to stop meditation once you have formed a connection with them, as future reflections allow you to gain more understanding of the runes in the future.

What is important to remember is that when you are performing runecasting, it is important to direct your thoughts. In the beginning, your focus might be brittle and capable of breaking off before it even holds on to the readings in front of you. Once you are able to calm the flow of thoughts in your mind, you may find that remembering the various aspects of the runes becomes easy.

The idea of meditation involves three aspects; the appearance of the rune, the feel of the rune in your hands, and the meaning of the rune. To meditate, find yourself a quiet spot where you won't be easily disturbed.

Now, close your eyes and imagine the rune. As you move your fingers over the rune, you send your energy across to it. Once you feel a comfortable flow within you, begin to think about the rune. Start with its basic properties. What is the rune's literal name? When you have thought of the name, ask yourself - what meaning can I derive from this name?

Next, focus on the rune's divination meanings. Do not worry if you are unable to remember them all. You can always perform this meditation again. Recollect as many of the words as possible. Try to think about each word and what it means in relation to the rune itself.

After this step, you will move on to its magic usages. Try to understand how this magic can benefit you or people in general.

Once you are done, think about what the rune is supposed to signify. What have you learned about the rune? What can it predict? How can its magical usages be used in many of its predictions? Is there more to this rune? What additional information can I add to the rune?

## Norse Mythology and Symbolism

Odin is the sacral high god of the Aesir. Within the mythology, there are two core groups of deities – the Aesir and the Vanir. The Aesir are predominantly gods of conscious actions such as war, death, language, and justice. The Vanir are associated with the natural cycles of life and fertility. Neither group is subservient to the other. The arrangement here is more representative of the need for union between the forces of natural cycles and fertility (Vanir) and those of conscious thought (Aesir). This is perhaps reflective of other symbols, such as the popular yin-yang figure. In Norse mythology, the concept of balance is quite popular.

# Elemental Links

One of the things you will learn, as well as apply in your rune readings, is the elemental attributions of each rune. There are four elements, which you might be aware of already. These are the elements of earth, air, water, and fire. Each of the 24 runes falls into one of the elements, showing their affinity for that particular element. This might become useful when you want to draw more meanings from your readings.

Historically, different runecasters link different runes to the elements. Because of this, you might not find a common technique to follow. However, the most widely accepted attributions are mentioned below. Remember to use the questions provided in this section to exercise your ideas about readings. As each element will have its own meaning, think about how well you can link them to your runecastings.

### *Earth*

This element is symbolic of solid foundations. It shows whether one has a firm grasp on reality. Along with this idea, the earth element also represents physical growth. You can use this idea during runecasting. When the runes are speaking to you about an idea, are you able to connect it to the idea of physical growth?

Another thing to note is that the earth represents steady growth. Perhaps that could be indicative of slow progress in the future.

Earth can also be attributed to Mother Earth. When you form this connection, you have many meanings in relation to motherhood, feminine qualities, the female form, and childbirth.

Earth may also represent the idea of being fixed to something. In other words, the person is rooted in a certain place and prefers not to travel much.

When it comes to the runes themselves, the following are the ones associated with the earth symbol; Uruz, Wunjo, Berkana, Othila, Isa, and Jera.

### *Water*

This element represents fluidity. This is an essential factor to consider when you are thinking about the fact that the person might be adaptive. This adaptiveness allows the individual to face many challenges in life. However, how can you relate this to the runes themselves?

Furthermore, water is representative of emotions. When you are casting runes, you might want to take into consideration this fact as you provide your readings. Think about the inner self of the individual and find out how the runes reflect their personality.

Kaunaz, Perth, Lagu, Ing, Raido, and Gebo are the runes that are associated with this element.

## *Air*

This element has strong connections with Odin. How can you associate this with the readings you have made so far?

Air is also the sign of taking in breath or, in other words, the act of inhaling life. If you equate this with your readings, is there a chance to show how the individual can discover life among the struggles in their life?

Air also represents the idea that your troubles can be carried away from you. Teiwaz, Berkana, Ehwaz, Algiz, Sowulo, and Mannaz are all runes of the air element.

## *Fire*

Fire represents the heat of passion. When you are working with this rune, perhaps you could make associations with sexual activity or eroticism.

This element also represents wrath. Use this to

speak about the conflicts in the individual's life and how they are dealing with it in a negative manner.

However, fire can also have a positive meaning. It is the element that spreads light, so it can reveal the fact that despite the struggles that the individual is likely to face, they may find light in the form of support, relationships, help, or even motivation.

Othila, Fehu, Thurisaz, Nauthiz, and Eihwaz are all runes of the fire element.

# The Nine World for Beginners

I have featured the Nine Realms as part of the divination process. But what are they exactly? How do they fit into the entire Norse mythological universe? I wanted to dive deeper into this in order to get more understanding about the mythology and help you form unique perspectives and understand how you can connect the runes to the realms.

In the mythology of Norse cosmology, the universe begins with a spark of fire from Muspellheim. This spark meets the primal ice waters of the realm of Niflheim — and its convergence creates the essential 'big bang' that creates the universe, which is also a theory formed by scientists. From this convergence, the resultant flow of energized water gives rise to the first beings—the proto-giant/god known as Ymir and the cosmic cow Audumbla.

Odin, Hoenir, and Lodur were three gods who were the sons of Bor and Bestla. Bor is similar to Ymir in that he has no paternal line and emerges forth from the ice waters of Niflheim as well. In order to bring structure and control to the universe, the brothers slay the proto-being Ymir and form the worlds from his body. The worlds align within the branches of the great tree Yggdrasil. The name Yggdrasil also translates as 'Ygg's steed'. The suggestion here is that Yggdrasil is the means of transport for a being named Ygg. Ygg itself translates to 'the terrible one' and Ygg is also the name of Odin. So, the implication is that the worlds align to make it easy for Odin to travel between them easily.

And finally, we come to the Nine Worlds of the Norse mythology:

Muspellheim—existed prior to the murder of Ymir and is the source of the primal energy that brings life into existence.

Nifelheim—also existed prior to the process that brought structure to the worlds. This icy cold land holds all potential.

Helheimr — the realm of the Goddess from whom its name takes its root. Helheimr is the land of those that have died of old age or disease and are now are under the care of Hel, daughter of Loki. Here, they can spend their time in the afterlife, share their knowledge with their descendants, or await reincarnation. Contrary to the entire horrific image created about Hel by Christian monks, the Goddess and her realm are quite clearly hospitable towards the dead. Who would have thought, right?

Svartalfheimr—this realm is the land of the underworld, beneath Midgard. Here, we can find the dwarven smiths of legends known as Weyland. These beings are responsible for the manifestation of energy. They are known to convert this energy into matter by manipulating atoms.

Jotunheim—this land is of the primal Jotun, a race of giants. The Jotun are some of the oldest, wisest, and strongest beings in existence. Some of them embody the concept of chaos. This chaos represents the ultimate potential for all things to manifest.

Ljossalfheimr — is the realm of the light elves, ruled over by Freyr, brother to Freyja. Here, we find the Alfar and Ljossalfar. The Alfar are enlightened souls that have once manifested as humans, whereas the Ljossalfar is a higher form of consciousness.

Asgard — this realm is the home of the Aesir-gods, the gods of consciousness, language and war.

Midgard— this the realm in which we live, also known as the realm of manifestation. This realm is the central axis point of the other eight worlds. Midgard is the crucible of Yggdrasil. Fire and ice meet in a clash, resulting in the creation of life.

# Tips to be successful with Divination

Finally, we will look at the very act of divination as we try to find out how we can be successful during our runecasting sessions. Please note that at this point, to become proficient with the runes themselves, you will need a considerable amount of practice. Of course, you can refer to the tips that we have provided in this book.

Please remember one thing. All the practice that you put into divination is actually a rather exciting and fun process. One tends to equate the idea of practice with stress, sleepless hours, and endless coffee breaks. However, this is not true.

If you are ready, let's dive into the ways in which you can become an excellent runecaster.

## *Record your sessions, at least when you are a beginner*

You must have noticed that I have provided tips on making notes about your sessions. This is important because you may not always have the best idea on how to proceed. You might make mistakes in the beginning or you may even be unsure about your readings. By looking back at your notes, you might find out your flaws and work on them. The more you record in the beginning, the less you will require it later on, especially when you are ready to try out the more advanced techniques of divination mentioned in this book.

Additionally, you might notice patterns in your work. These could help you try out different approaches to runecasting and reading. You may even develop your own unique techniques to read for someone else. All of this will help you grow, develop your own runecaster persona, and give you the confidence to provide an incredible reading.

### *Meditate*

I cannot stress the importance of meditation enough. During the initial stages, runecasting can be rather heavy on the mind. This might dishearten you or in some cases, leave you exhausted. You need to keep your spirits up. To do this, try and find time to meditate regularly. Once you get used to divination, you will be able to absorb new knowledge, work with runes, perform fluid readings, and even practice advanced techniques with relative ease. The road to mastery is riddled with many meditations.

Additionally, I would also recommend meditating

after a reading session. This will clear your head of any influence of the previous session and put you in the right frame of mind for future sessions.

I recommend simple breathing exercises, so you do not need to perform complex meditative routines.

### *Be grounded in reality*
Here is a simple visualization technique that you can use to ground yourself to the present. Find a quiet spot where you won't be disturbed. Now close your eyes and begin breathing slowly. Inhale while counting to five. Then, exhale while counting to six. Perform this routine a few times.
Now, bring your breathing back to a normal level. Imagine the roots of a tree. Imagine that these roots are attached to your body. They are digging deep into the earth and are holding you down. They have grounded you.

Start breathing and deeply inhale while counting to five, then exhale while counting to six. Perform this a few times. When you are ready, open your eyes and feel the presence of the room. Look around you and notice all the details of the space you are in.

Whenever you feel stressed or overwhelmed, simply perform this routine to clear your mind

and be ready to perform your reading with clarity
and understanding.

### *Do not multitask*

Keep all items and sources of distraction away
from you. You will not need your phone or other
personal items. Make time for the reading. If you
feel that you might receive a call that is rather
urgent, try finding another time to perform the
reading, when you might not be interrupted. Do
not multitask as your mind might be divided
towards two focus points. Additionally,
divination is a method that requires you to have a
higher degree of concentration. You must be
totally focused on the task at hand to be able to
tap into your reservoir of knowledge, abilities,
and experiences.

### *Be patient*

The answers may not always come to you
immediately. Give yourself the time to wait for
them to come. If you feel that you have been
trying too hard and you are still unable to find the
answers, go ahead and take a break. Take ten
minutes for a quick meditation session. For this
meditation, all you have to do is find a nice, quiet
spot where you will not be disturbed. Sit down,
close your eyes, and take a few quick deep

breaths. You might notice a flood of thoughts entering your mind. Do not be alarmed. Mentally note down the fact that there is a thought in your mind and then discard it. Continue doing this until your mind feels clear and you feel calm. Then, get back to your reading and see if you notice any difference.

Sometimes, you might need to stop the reading entirely. This happens especially to beginners. When you find yourself in a mental rut, do not continue further. Take your notes with you and see what you have accomplished so far. If you need to make any changes to your approach to reading, this would be the best time to do so.

Remember the adage - practice makes perfect. Try not to get too frustrated at not being able to perform divination successfully; runecasters of legends might have also experienced such situations.

### *Do not influence the answers*
As tempting as it may seem, do not try to force the answers into existence. Allow them to come to you. By compelling yourself to form answers, you might not learn anything new. Also, they might give you the wrong readings. In order to avoid such situations, keep your mind focused on the task. Go through the steps of the reading

slowly and in complete awareness. If you are unsure of a step, take the time to think about it. If you need some guidance, always refer to this book for help. When you are ready, go back to your reading.

Also, I advise you to try and remove emotions from your reading. It is easy to be emotionally affected sometimes. While having a sense of feeling regarding a reading is human, too much emotion might compel you to act in a particular manner. You might try to force a more favorable outcome, or could even try to make it unfavorable.

Keep an objective state of mind, and your readings should be fine.

# Final thoughts

Reading is an exciting journey, and this includes the entire process of learning the lore and mythology, finding out about the runes and creating them yourself, and practicing runecasting.

Remember that there are no fixed answers. Keep your mind open. Be patient and work on your runic knowledge. Before long, you might find yourself becoming the next runemaster.

As parting words, I would like to leave you with this message. See if you can find out what it means.

***Vivienne Grant***

# Bibliography

Language - Language and culture. (2019). Retrieved from https://www.britannica.com/topic/language/Language-and-culture

Fischer, S. (2001). A history of writing. London: Reaktion.

Why are humans so much smarter than other primates? | Genetic Literacy Project. (2019). Retrieved from https://geneticliteracyproject.org/2018/09/24/why-are-humans-so-much-smarter-than-other-primates/

Elephants Have The Most Neurons. Why Aren't They The Smartest Animals?. (2019). Retrieved from https://www.forbes.com/sites/quora/2018/09/12/elephants-have-the-most-neurons-why-arent-they-the-smartest-animals/#56c7e7786afb

When Other Species Are Smarter. (2019). Retrieved from https://www.psychologytoday.com/us/blog/the-human-beast/201803/when-other-species-are-smarter

How many languages are there in the world? |

Linguistic Society of America. (2019). Retrieved from https://www.linguisticsociety.org/content/how-many-languages-are-there-world

How many words are there in the Engli... | Oxford Dictionaries. (2019). Retrieved from https://en.oxforddictionaries.com/explore/how-many-words-are-there-in-the-english-language/

Ethnologue: Languages of the World. (2019). Retrieved from https://www.ethnologue.com/

What do Pagans believe?. (2019). Retrieved from http://www.bbc.co.uk/religion/0/20693321

Odin's Discovery of the Runes - Norse Mythology for Smart People. (2019). Retrieved from https://norse-mythology.org/tales/odins-discovery-of-the-runes/

Thorsson, E. (2012). Runelore. San Francisco, Calif.: Weiser Books.

Martin-Clarke, D. The Hávamál.

The Earliest Known Runic Inscription : HistoryofInformation.com. (2019). Retrieved from http://www.historyofinformation.com/detail.php?entryid=3095

Thorsson, E. (2012). Futhark, a Handbook of Rune Magic. Weiser Books.

(2019). Retrieved from https://blackwitchcoven.com/wp-content/uploads/2015/09/A-Practical-Guide-to-the-Runes.pdf

&raquo;, M. (2019). How to Make Rune Staves. Retrieved from https://www.instructables.com/id/How-to-Make-Rune-Staves/

Thorsson, E. (1990). At the Well of Wyrd. York Beach, Me.: Samuel Weiser.

Runecasting Layouts. (2019). Retrieved from http://www.sunnyway.com/runes/layouts.html

(2019). Retrieved from https://whisperingwood.homestead.com/Rune_Course.pdf

Mountfort, P. (2003). Nordic runes. Rochester, Vt.: Destiny Books.

Peschel, L. (1999). A practical guide to the runes. St. Paul, Minn.: Llewellyn Publications.

Thorsson, E. The big book of runes and rune magic.